T0328478

Cambridge Elements

Elements in Corporate Governance
edited by
Thomas Clarke
UTS Business School, University of Technology Sydney

THE EVOLUTION OF CORPORATE GOVERNANCE

Bob Tricker
University of Oxford

CAMBRIDGE
UNIVERSITY PRESS

CAMBRIDGE
UNIVERSITY PRESS

University Printing House, Cambridge CB2 8BS, United Kingdom

One Liberty Plaza, 20th Floor, New York, NY 10006, USA

477 Williamstown Road, Port Melbourne, VIC 3207, Australia

314–321, 3rd Floor, Plot 3, Splendor Forum, Jasola District Centre,
New Delhi – 110025, India

79 Anson Road, #06–04/06, Singapore 079906

Cambridge University Press is part of the University of Cambridge.

It furthers the University's mission by disseminating knowledge in the pursuit of
education, learning, and research at the highest international levels of excellence.

www.cambridge.org
Information on this title: www.cambridge.org/9781108965422
DOI: 10.1017/9781108974653

First published 2020

A catalogue record for this publication is available from the British Library.

ISBN 978-1-108-96542-2 Paperback
ISSN 2515–7175 (online)
ISSN 2515–7167 (print)

The Evolution of Corporate Governance

Elements in Corporate Governance

DOI: 10.1017/9781108974653
First published online: November 2020

Bob Tricker
University of Oxford
Author for correspondence: Bob Tricker, bobtricker@aol.com

Abstract: In this Element the origins of corporate governance are reviewed, recognising that corporate entities have always been governed, that important developments took place in the seventeenth and eighteenth centuries, and the huge significance of the invention of the joint-stock limited liability company. The development of corporate governance in the twentieth century around the world is explored, with complex groups, private companies and top management dominating shareholder power appearing in the inter-war years. Some unresolved issues in both principle and practice are identified. Various theories of corporate governance are described and contrasted. The subject is seen to be in search of its paradigm and a systems theoretical relationship between the theories is suggested. The need to rethink the concept of the limited liability company is argued, and a call is made for the development of a philosophy of corporate governance.

Keywords: corporate governance, evolution, institutions, limited liability company, management

ISBNs: 9781108965422 (PB), 9781108974653 (OC)
ISSNs: 2515-7175 (online), 2515-7167 (print)

Contents

1 Introduction

The phrase 'corporate governance' came into prominence in the 1990s, following the publication in the United Kingdom of the Cadbury Report[1] (1992). The research journal *Corporate Governance – An International Review*[2] was founded in the same year. But the need for corporate entities to be governed can be traced far back into the history of trade: back through the regulation imposed by the United States Securities and Exchange Commission[3] since 1934, the brilliant invention of the limited liability company in the nineteenth century, which led to the burgeoning vast, complex and rapidly changing world of corporate governance today, right back to medieval times when promoters of a venture had to delegate supervision to others.

This Element traces the evolution of the concept of corporate governance from those early times to its present-day role of setting objectives, strategies and policies, supervising management and ensuring accountability that are essential in every corporate entity. Economic history, culture and even religion will be shown to have influenced the development of approaches to corporate governance around the world.

Previous attempts to chart the evolution of corporate governance have tended to cite research papers published in refereed journals, often those published in the USA. This produces a myopic perspective because, to date, research has brought few changes to corporate governance practice around the world. As will be shown in this Element, significant change to corporate governance policies and practices have been responses to perceived needs, often reflecting economic failure or corporate collapse.

Although many of the underlying legal concepts of corporate governance still owe more to their mid-nineteenth-century origins than to the realities of complex, modern business situations and risks, developments have often been responses to corporate collapses rather than developments in theory. Nevertheless, the range of theoretical insights will be considered; and contemporary frontiers of the subject identified.

This Element reviews the way corporate governance has evolved over centuries to this day. It endeavours to identify the cause of significant changes in corporate governance policy and practice, as well as topics

---

[1] Cadbury, Sir Adrian (1992) *The Financial Aspects of Corporate Governance: a Report of the Committee on Corporate Governance.* Gee & Co., London.

[2] *Corporate Governance – An International Review,* Volume 1, Number 1, January 1993, Blackwell Publishers, Oxford.

[3] The Securities Exchange Act (1934) Pub.L.73–291, 48 Stat. 881, to regulate the governance of companies listed on US stock markets and the trading of their shares, bonds and debentures.

that are on the frontiers of the subject. The development of theory about corporate governance is discussed, with its recognition as a subject worthy of serious study. The lack of clear corporate governance paradigms is considered, and a call made for a philosophy of this important new subject.

2 The Origins of Corporate Governance

Corporate Entities Have Always Been Governed

Chaucer (*c.*1343–1400) was the first to record the word 'governance'[4] although he was not sure how it should be spelled.[5] At that time, of course, it was a city or state that needed governing. Nevertheless, although the use of the phrase 'corporate governance' is recent, the need for governance of trade ventures is ancient. Shakespeare (1564–1616) understood the challenge. Antonio, his Merchant of Venice[6], agonised as he watched his ships sail out of sight, knowing that his fortune was now in the hands of others.

Whenever a principal relies on agents to look after his interests, governance issues arise. This agency dilemma has long been recognised. Shareholders in a company elect their board directors to look after their interests. Members of professional bodies elect their council. Members of a club appoint their committee. All corporate entities need a governing body nominated and elected in line with that organisation's constitution.

These governing bodies have a variety of names. For companies it is usually the board of directors. For other organisations it may be the 'council' or the 'committee'. The Bank of England has a 'Court', reflecting its ancient origins. Oxford colleges, with classical simplicity, often call their governing body 'the governing body': surprisingly not '*corpus governate*'.

Corporate Governance in the Seventeenth and Eighteenth Centuries

Economic competition accompanied by political and military strife, grew during the seventeenth century between Britain, Holland, Portugal and Spain, each with ambitions of empire. In 1600, the East India Company was created with a monopoly over all trade between England and Asia, under a royal charter granted by Queen Elizabeth I. The Company was a joint-stock company, with over 1,000 stockholders, who elected a governing board of twenty-four directors each year. The company traded principally with India

---

[4] Troilus and Criseyde.   [5] 'gouernance' or 'governaunce'.
[6] Shakespeare, William (1598) *The Merchant of Venice, Act 1 Scene 1* 'In sooth, I know not why I am so sad . . .'.

and China in cotton, silk, tea and opium, at one time administering parts of the British Indian Empire with its own private army.[7] The Dutch East India Company was granted a charter by the Republic of the Netherlands in 1602 to run Dutch colonies and to trade with Asia.[8] The Dutch West India Company was chartered in 1621, to run the slave trade between Africa, the Caribbean and North America. The Hudson Bay Company received its royal charter in 1670, when Prince Rupert, cousin of England's King Charles II, wanted to pursue fur trading in what is now Canada.

In 1711 a company was incorporated in England to trade with Spain's South American colonies, mainly in slaves. The story of the South Sea Company marked a turning point in public attitude to corporate business. In 1718, King George 1 became a governor of the company, bringing prestige and public confidence. In 1720, the British House of Lords incredibly gave the South Sea Company a monopoly on the premise that the company would guarantee the British national debt. Massive speculation in the company's shares followed. Then the bubble burst. Members of the British aristocracy lost their fortunes, banks failed, while directors of the company were imprisoned and their wealth confiscated. The Chancellor of the Exchequer was found to have taken bribes to promote the company's stock. There was a public outcry about such speculation and excessive corporate risk-taking.

The evolution of corporate governance has since been influenced by other examples of dubious business models and unrealistic risk-taking, as we shall see in Enron[9] following the global financial crisis (2007–10)[10].

Adam Smith (1723–90), a moral philosopher at the University of Glasgow, often considered the father of modern economics,[11] commented on corporate behaviour offering a classic corporate governance perspective:

> The directors of companies, being the managers of other people's money rather than their own, cannot well be expected to watch over it with the same anxious vigilance with which [they] watch over their own.

---

[7] Stern, Philip (2019) English East India Company-State and the Modern Corporation: the Google of its Time? in T. Clarke, J. O'Brien and C. O'Kelley, *The Oxford Handbook of the Corporation*. Oxford University Press, Oxford, 75–92.

[8] Frentrop, P. (2019) The Dutch East India Company: the First Corporate Governance Debacle, in T. Clarke, J. O'Brien and C. O'Kelley, *The Oxford Handbook of the Corporation*. Oxford University Press, Oxford, 51–74.

[9] Enron was a major US energy company that metamorphosed into a financial institution, trading energy futures without the board realising that the company's risk profile had changed fundamentally.

[10] When companies failed and banks had to be bailed out by governments.

[11] Smith, Adam (1776; 1976) *The Wealth of Nations*, rev. ed., George J. Stigler (ed.). University of Chicago Press, Chicago.

The Invention of the Limited Liability Company

As the eighteenth century moved into the industrial revolution of the nineteenth, there were only three basic structures available to a business, other than corporations created under charter from the monarch or the state: a sole trader; a partnership; or through an unincorporated corporate entity. In each of these structures, creditors could pursue their debts with the owners. This could mean that ultimately anyone investing in a business faced bankruptcy. In those days, failure to meet your debts was a crime, which could lead to debtors' prison, with the possibility of the family being sent to the parish workhouse.

Clearly, unless you were directly involved in controlling the enterprise, there was little incentive for sleeping partners or non-management investors to risk their capital. Yet this was exactly what was needed by businesses in a period of economic growth, generated by the industrial revolution. Firms needed external capital to expand faster than the founders' capital and ploughed-back profits would allow. Moreover, an emerging middle class had funds available. What was needed was a means of investing in a business without becoming responsible for its debts.

A form of corporate incorporation that limited the liability of investors for a company's debts was created in France in 1807 – the *Société en commandité par Actions*.[12] However, in the French model the protection of the law only applied to external investors *not* involved in the management of the enterprise. Executive directors and managers holding shares were still vulnerable.

In Britain, the need for a form of incorporation that could raise capital without exposing the investors financially grew. Parliament debated the issue and there were calls for the creation of an incorporation that followed the French design. However, the Limited Liability Act (1855)[13] gave limited liability to *all* shareholders, whether they were involved in the management of the company or not, although the records of the parliamentary debates suggest that some Members of Parliament thought they were adopting the French model. The Companies Act (1862)[14] reinforced this form of corporate incorporation.

The joint-stock limited liability company became one of the most successful systems ever designed. Under the dictates of company law, a legal entity is created distinct from its owners. This corporate entity has many of the legal rights of a real person: to contract; sue and be sued; own property; and employ people. However, the shareholders only risk their equity investment. They are

---

[12] Freedeman, Charles E. (1979) *Joint-Stock Enterprise in France 1807–1867 – From Privileged Company to Modern Corporation*. The University of North Carolina Press, Chapel Hill, NC.

[13] The Limited Liability Act, 18 and 19 VICT. a. 183.

[14] The Companies Act, VICT CAP.LXXXIX 7 August 1862. 'An Act for the Incorporation, Regulation, and Winding-up of Trading Companies and other Associations.'

not responsible for corporate debt, unlike the owners of an unincorporated entity.

A company has a life of its own, giving continuity beyond the life of its founders. Shares in the company can be bought and sold. Nevertheless, share ownership is the basis of power over a company. In principle, shareholders elect their directors. Those directors owe a duty of stewardship to their shareholders to whom they are accountable.

The huge success of this opportunity to incorporate companies with limited shareholder liability led the writers of the Savoy operas, Gilbert and Sullivan (1893)[15] to satirise the trend in their opera *Utopia, Limited*.

> All hail, astonishing fact,
> All hail, invention new,
> The Joint Stock Company Act of Parliament Sixty-two.
> And soon or late I always call for Stock Exchange quotation.
> No scheme too great, and none too small for companification.

In America, some states enacted laws to facilitate the incorporation of companies. In the years following the American Civil War (1861–5), many companies were incorporated, some quite significant in the railroad, steel, manufacturing and other major industries. The New York Stock Exchange was founded in 1817 and Wall Street traded shares in these new public companies, raising capital to fund their growth. But the investors' liability was not yet limited. Most state company law regulated companies tightly, requiring each company to describe its objectives and, significantly, to give it a finite lifespan. A further restriction was that one company could not own another.

Subsequently, state constitutions were amended and laws rewritten to be more amenable to increasingly powerful companies. Shareholder limited liability was introduced. Charter battles were fought to allow corporate groups, in which companies could own other companies. Eventually, corporate charters no longer limited the range of companies' activities and their lifespans.

In 1918, in what is often considered a landmark case,[16] the right of individual states to regulate institutions in their jurisdiction was challenged at the federal level. The courts in the state of New Hampshire had revoked the Royal Charter given to Dartmouth College by King George III of England. But the US Supreme Court overruled the lower courts. Many states saw this as a federal attack on state sovereignty and rewrote their laws to circumvent the Dartmouth ruling (Friedman 1973).[17] To this day companies in the United States are

---

[15] Gilbert, Arthur and Sullivan, W. S. *Utopia, Limited*, D'Oyly Carte Opera Company, 1893.

[16] *Trustees of Dartmouth College* v. *Woodward* (1819).

[17] Friedman, Lawrence M. (1973) *A History of American Law*. Simon and Schuster, New York.

incorporated at the state not the federal level. But state company laws vary, which is why many US companies incorporate in the state of Delaware, a jurisdiction supportive of corporate entities.

In the late nineteenth and early twentieth centuries, the British Empire spread the concept of the limited liability company around the world. The company laws of Australia, Canada, some Caribbean islands that are now tax havens, Hong Kong, India, Malaya (now Malaysia), New Zealand, Singapore, South Africa and some other African countries still reflect those origins; although subsequently their company law evolved to meet local circumstances. However, even today, case law made in courts throughout the British Commonwealth of Nations may provide precedents in other member countries, and some retain the ultimate right of appeal to the British Privy Council. Hong Kong, which became a Special Administrative Region of China in 1997, still retains its British-orientated legal system and company law, although the right of final appeal has shifted from London to Beijing.

The basic idea of the limited liability company was starkly simple and proved superbly successful. Industrial innovation and expansion, growth in employment, and economic wealth followed worldwide. However, the success of the simple mid-nineteenth-century model led to growing complexity, although the original corporate concept still underpins contemporary company law.

3 The Development of Corporate Governance in the Twentieth Century

Inter-war Years: Private Companies, Top Management Domination

Originally, all joint-stock limited liability companies were public companies. In other words, they were incorporated to raise capital from the public. By the early twentieth century, however, it was recognised that the model could be used to give limited liability to family firms and other private enterprises, even though they did not need access to external capital. Today, of course, private companies vastly outnumber public companies.

Directors also realised that companies could acquire shares in other companies and, if they held the majority voting equity, control them. This led, in economically advanced countries, to complex groups in which the holding company owned a pyramid of subsidiary companies held at different levels.

The ownership of companies listed on stock markets had also changed. In the early days, shareholders tended to be wealthy individuals who could attend or be represented at shareholder meetings. But by the early years of the twentieth century things were changing. As many listed companies became large and complex, so did their shareholder base, which could now be numerous and geographically widespread. Private investors were being overshadowed by institutional investors: pension funds, financial institutions, hedge funds and private equity firms. The objectives of these investors differed in both their strategic time horizons and their expectations about dividends and capital growth. Chains of financial intermediaries could also stand between companies and their investors. Shareholders in major companies had become distant from the boardrooms of the companies they owned.

Using data from companies in the United States, Berle and Means (1932)[18] drew attention to the growing separation of power between the executive management of major public companies and their increasingly diverse and remote shareholders. They realised the significance of corporate power, observing that:

> The rise of the modern corporation has brought a concentration of economic power which can compete on equal terms with the modern state – economic power versus political power, each strong in its own field. The state seeks, in some aspects, to regulate the corporation, while the corporation, steadily becoming more powerful, makes every effort to avoid such regulation ... The future may see the economic organism, now typified by the corporation, not only on an equal plane with the state, but possibly even superseding it as the dominant form of social organisation.

Berle and Means' work made a seminal contribution to corporate governance thinking; although that was not a phrase they knew. But it was to take a long time for their intellectual inheritance to be recognised. For the next forty years, the work of directors and boards remained the province of jurisprudence, enlivened by anecdote and exhortation.

The 1970s: Audit Committees, Two-tier Boards and Stakeholder Responsibilities

In 1971, a pioneering work by Mace[19], based on research in US companies, tried to establish what directors really did. His findings challenged conventional wisdom:

> In most companies, boards of directors serve as a source of advice and counsel, serve as some sort of discipline, and act in crisis situations if the president dies suddenly or is asked to resign because of unsatisfactory management performance.

---

[18] Berle, Adolf A. and Means, Gardiner C. (1932) *The Modern Corporation and Private Property*. Macmillan, rev. by Adolf Berle (1967), Columbia University, Harcourt, Brace and World, New York.

[19] Mace, Myles L. (1971) *Directors: Myth and Reality*. Division of Research, Graduate School of Business Administration, Harvard University, Boston, MA.

The business literature describing the classical functions of boards of directors typically includes three important roles:

1. establishing basic objectives, corporate strategies, and board policies;
2. asking discerning questions;
3. selecting the president.

[Instead] I found that boards of directors of most large and medium-sized companies do not establish objectives, strategies, and policies however defined. These roles are performed by company management. Presidents and outside directors generally agreed that only management can and should have these responsibilities.

A second classical role assigned to boards of directors is that of asking discerning questions – inside and outside the board meetings. Again, it was found that directors do not, in fact, do this. Board meetings are not regarded as proper forums for discussions arising out of questions asked by board members.

A third classical role usually regarded as a responsibility of the board of directors is the selection of the president. Yet it was found that in most companies, directors do not in fact select the president, except in ... crisis situations.

Interest in the work of boards of directors developed further in the 1970s. In the United States, in 1972, the Securities and Exchange Commission required listed companies to create audit committees as standing committees of the main board comprising independent outside directors. These audit committees were to provide a bridge between the external auditor and the main board, ensuring that directors were made aware of any issues that had arisen between the auditor and the company's finance department. Mautz and Neumann (1970, 1977)[20] discussed the practicalities of audit committees being introduced in the United States. Auerbach (1973)[21] described these audit committees as: 'a new corporate institution'.

In the United Kingdom, Tricker (1978)[22] studied board membership in British companies, intending to advocate audit committees for the United Kingdom. However, he found that although many listed company boards *did* have non-executive directors, they tended to be a minority and the concept of director independence was not understood. The conventional wisdom seemed to

---

[20] Mautz, R. K. and Neumann, F. L. (1970) The effective corporate audit committee. *Harvard Business Review*, November/December, 57–65.
   Mautz, R. K. and Neumann, F. L. (1977) *Corporate Audit Committees: Policies and Practices*. Ernst and Ernst, New York.

[21] Auerbach, Norman E. (1973) Audit committees: new corporate institution. *Financial Executive*, September, 96–7,102, 104.

[22] Tricker, R. I. (1978) *The Independent Director: a Study of the Non-executive Director and of the Audit Committee*, Tolley with Deloitte, Haskins & Sells, London.

be that while non-executive directors could provide useful inputs to board discussions, their role was not to provide a check on the executive directors. Consequently, Tricker concluded that audit committees, based on the US model, would not work in the United Kingdom. Sir Brandon Rhys-Williams, a British member of parliament, did call for non-executive directors and audit committees in the United Kingdom, a proposal that led to a green paper – *The Conduct of Company Directors* (1977) – and a parliamentary bill calling for audit committees. It failed in parliament.

In the United States, an increasingly litigious climate saw shareholders seeking recompense from directors, boards and auditors of listed companies and auditors for alleged losses they had incurred. Auditors were particularly at risk, because it was thought that their indemnity insurance provided a 'deep pocket'. The focus on board-level checks and balances increased.

The European Economic Community (EEC),[23] trying to harmonise company law throughout all member states, issued a series of draft directives. The EEC draft fifth directive (1972) proposed that unitary boards, with both executive and non-executive outside directors, used in the United Kingdom and elsewhere in the EEC, be replaced by two-tier boards, as used in Germany and Holland.

In the two-tier board system, companies have two distinct boards. The upper supervisory board has only non-executive directors, who monitor and oversee the work of the lower executive board, which is comprised entirely of executive directors, who run the business. No common membership is allowed. The supervisory board has the power to hire and fire members of the executive board.

The EEC proposal for two-tier boards was not well received in Britain. First, it was argued, at least by directors, that unitary boards worked well. Second, the EEC directive also called for worker directors on the supervisory board. This followed the idea of co-determination, a long-standing tradition in Germany. In this model, the company was thought of as a social partnership between capital and labour with the supervisory board made up of equal numbers of representatives of the shareholders and the employees.

The United Kingdom's response was the report of a committee chaired by Alan Bullock,[24] Master of St. Catherine's College Oxford. *The Report of the Committee of Inquiry on Industrial Democracy (1977)*[25] and the research papers (1976) associated with it reflected the first serious proposals on board structure in Britain. The committee proposed a continuation of the unitary board, but with

---

[23] Subsequently the EEC became the European Union (EU).

[24] Later to be Sir Alan then Lord Bullock.

[25] *Committee of Inquiry on Industrial Democracy (the Bullock Report)*, Hansard, 23 February 1977, volume 380, cc179–355.

some directors representing the employees of the company, elected through their trade unions. The Bullock Report was also not well received in British boardrooms and was not pursued.

During the 1970s, reports from inspectors appointed by the UK Department of Trade suggested corporate governance problems, although that phrase itself was yet to appear. The report into Pergamon Press (1971) concluded that founder Robert Maxwell should not again run a public company; advice that was subsequently ignored, enabling him to build a media empire that collapsed dramatically twenty years later. Other inquiries, which examined board-level problems at Rolls Royce (1973), London and County Securities (1976) and Lonrho Ltd (1976), added to the interest in the way companies were governed, although commentators at the time wrote about the way they were managed.

Another striking development during the decade of the 1970s was the questioning of the social responsibility of business in society. Broadly, the concern was whether major companies had responsibilities beyond their legal duty to their shareholders. It was widely recognised that all companies had to satisfy their customers and, in the process, provide employment, opportunities for suppliers, and contribute to society by paying their taxes. But the classical nineteenth-century model of the joint-stock limited liability company was unequivocal: the prime duty of directors was to their investors, who had elected them, and to act as stewards of those shareholders' investment.

However, given the scale and significance of many companies, some argued that directors should report to and, some believed, be accountable to a range of stakeholders who could be affected by board decisions – customers, employees, suppliers and others in the supply chain, the local community and the state.

The American Bar Association, which had been considering alternative bases of power over companies,[26] clashed with the Corporate Roundtable, which represented directors, who were convinced of the merits of the existing stewardship model. Jensen and Meckling (1976),[27] in an article that was to provide the foundation for corporate governance agency theory, questioned whether the classical concept of the company could survive.

In a much quoted and sometimes misquoted paper, Friedman (1970)[28] claimed in the title of his paper that:

---

[26] Small, Marshall L. (2011) The 1970s: the committee on corporate laws joins the corporate governance debate, The Model Business Corporation Act at Sixty, *Law and Contemporary Problems*, 74(Winter), 129–36, Duke University, Durham, NC.

[27] Jensen, Michael C. and William H. Meckling (1976) *Theory of the firm: Managerial behavior, agency costs and ownership structure,* Journal of Financial Economics, Volume 3, Issue 4, October 1976, Pages 305-360

[28] Friedman, Milton (1970), The social responsibility of business is to increase its profits. *New York Times Magazine*, September 13.

The social responsibility of business is to increase its profits ... businessmen, who talk this way, are unwitting puppets of the intellectual forces that have been undermining the basis of a free society these past decades. The discussions of the 'social responsibilities of business' are notable for their analytical looseness and lack of rigor ... In his capacity as a corporate executive, the manager is the agent of the individuals who own the corporation or establish the eleemosynary[29] institution, and his primary responsibility is to them.

Friedman concluded his thesis:

There is one and only one social responsibility of business – to use its resources and engage in activities designed to increase its profits so long as it stays within the rules of the game, which is to say, engages in open and free competition without deception or fraud.

Friedman made a seminal contribution to corporate governance thinking, which underpinned agency theory, subsequently the largest contributor to the corporate governance research literature. As we will see, the principle of shareholder primacy is increasingly being questioned.

In the United Kingdom a committee of the Confederation of British Industry (CBI), chaired by Lord Watkinson (1973), published a report[30] on the responsibilities of the British public company, which recognised the significance of stakeholders to corporate success. In a similar vein, Fogarty (1975)[31] discussed companies' responsibilities and stakeholder participation.

A discussion paper[32] *The Corporate Report* was published in 1975, which called for all 'economic entities' to report regularly and publicly to all those who might be affected by corporate activities. Moreover, the paper suggested that companies should be accountable to these stakeholders for their decisions. Such a dramatic shift of reporting, accountability and control, and the inevitable dilution of shareholder and board power was enough to consign these proposals to the top shelf of the archives.

The 1980s: Directors Misbehave, Corporate Governance Named

During the 1980s, under the economic policies of Reagan in the United States and Thatcher in the United Kingdom, directors' attention was focused on increasing shareholder value. In the United Kingdom, many previously

---

[29] 'eleemosynary' = a charity organization.

[30] Confederation of British Industry (1973) *The Responsibilities of the British Public Company: Final Report of the Company Affairs Committee*. CBI, London.

[31] Fogarty, Michael P. (1975) *Company Responsibility and Participation: a New Agenda*. PEP Broadsheet No. 554, Vol. XLI, August, London.

[32] The Accounting Standards Steering Committee (1975) *The Corporate Report*. The Institute of Chartered Accountants in England and Wales, London.

nationalised entities – coal, electricity, gas, railways and water – were re-privatised. Entities that had been state-owned and controlled were now in private ownership.

Throughout the economically developed world, boards of public companies faced potential hostile bids for control of their companies from predators, sometimes funded by newly available high-yield, high-risk 'junk' bonds. In the United States, massive deals, based on the misuse of insider information, through finance house Drexel Burnham Lambert, enshrined the names of Ivan Boesky, Michael Levine and Michael Milken in corporate governance history.

In Japan, Nomura Securities was accused of being too closely allied with its financial regulator, having offered well-paid sinecures to senior bureaucrats when they retired: a practice known in Japan as '*amakudari* ' or 'descent from heaven'. Lavish payouts to major institutional clients to meet their losses and payments to underworld syndicates, '*yakuza*', to prevent their interference in company meetings were also alleged. The presidents of Nomura Securities and Nikko Securities resigned; as did Nomura's chairman, who also stood down from vice-chair of the '*Keidanren*', the federation of Japanese economic organisations.

In Australia, a 1989 report by the National Companies and Securities Commission[33] on the collapse of Rothwells Ltd, a listed financial institution, commented that 'at no time did the board of the company perform its duties satisfactorily'. The company was dominated by entrepreneur Laurie Connell, who provided loans to companies on the second board of the Western Australia Stock Exchange that were newer, smaller and inevitably riskier than those on the main board. Connell provided funds to such dubious projects that he acquired the title 'Last Chance Laurie'. The auditors refused to sign the 1988 company accounts, and the official report disclosed 'massive private drawings by Connell' without disclosure to the other directors. The stock-market collapse in 1987 finally ended the Rothwell saga. Another Australian caught up in Rothwell was Alan Bond – a truly remarkable man – voted Australia's man of the year in 1978, he sponsored Australia's yachting that seized the America's Cup in 1983, and in 1987 he bought Van Gogh's painting *Irises* for $54million (the highest price ever paid for a single painting). But in 1992, he was declared bankrupt and jailed on corruption charges relating to the syphoning of funds from Bell Resources to his own company the Bond Corporation. In 1996, he was jailed again on fraud charges concerning Bond Corporation. Yet by 2008 he was listed among Australia's 200 richest men.

---

[33] Now the Australian Securities Commission.

During the 1980s, boards of listed companies in the United States came under pressure from their institutional investors, who demanded better performance and longer-term strategic information. Directors of American Express, General Motors and IBM found institutional fund managers voting their shares against boards whom they considered to be performing badly. Demand also grew for an end to governance practices that protected companies and their incumbent boards from the likelihood of hostile takeover bids. Companies needed institutional investor support to tap the growing pension fund and savings funds. Investigative media and the threat of litigation added to the pressure on directors in America.

The US Treadway Commission[34] was formed in 1985 to consider fraudulent corporate financial reporting. Its first report (1987) made recommendations to the Securities and Exchange Commission and to boards of directors. It also led to the creation of the Committee of Sponsoring Organisations of the Treadway Commission (COSO)[35], a private-sector initiative to encourage more effective business activities. In the United Kingdom, four directors of the drinks company Guinness were convicted of scheming to inflate the price of their company to finance a bid for the Scottish drinks company Distillers. In another noteworthy case, Robert Maxwell, who dominated two listed companies, had raided their pension funds to finance private ventures.[36]

Boards dominated by powerful executive directors were now seen to need checks and balances, through strong independent directors. Where the posts of chief executive and chairman of the board were combined, as happened in some prominent US companies, the need was particularly acute. The concepts of corporate governance were at last to become the focus of attention; indeed, the phrase itself was about to appear. Official inquiries, launched following company failures, alleged board-level excesses and apparently dominant chief executives, which led to new corporate regulations and developments in company law.

---

[34] Officially the National Commission on Fraudulent Financial Reporting is known by the name of its chairman, former SEC Commissioner James C. Treadway, Jr. The Treadway Commission was funded by the American Institute of Certified Public Accountants (AICPA), the American Accounting Association (AAA), the Financial Executive Institute (FEI), the Institute of Internal Auditors (IIA) and the National Association of Accountants (NAA).

[35] The Committee of Sponsoring Organizations (COSO) of the Treadway Commission is a voluntary private-sector organisation dedicated to guiding executive management and governance participants towards the establishment of more effective, efficient and ethical business operations on a global basis. It has published concepts and frameworks, including frameworks for risk management and internal control.

[36] Clarke, Thomas (1992) The business descent of Robert Maxwell. *Media Culture and Society*, Sage, London, 14(May), 463–73; Clarke, Thomas (1993) Case study: Robert Maxwell: master of corporate malfeasance. *Corporate Governance: An International Review*, 1(3): 141–51.

During the 1980s, research also began to contribute to the subject and gave it a name. Mintzberg (1984)[37] explored whether it was any longer feasible for major public companies to be controlled by their shareholders. Tricker (1984)[38] wrote about the structure of boards and complex corporate groups on British listed companies. The scale and complexity of corporate groups had continued to grow, with groups of more than 250 subsidiaries, with chains of subsidiary companies covering seven or eight levels. This book used the title *Corporate Governance*.

Baysinger and Butler (1985), using the phrase 'corporate governance', looked at the effects on corporate performance of changes in board composition. In 1988, the Financial Executives Research Foundation[39] published an annotated bibliography of corporate governance with just 74 pages: today, a Google request for 'corporate governance' accesses many million references.

The 1990s – Corporate Regulation, Voluntary Codes

Up to now, commentators had tended to distinguish two basic models of corporate governance: the Anglo-American model with unitary boards comprising both executive directors and outside, non-executive directors; and the European or German two-tier model, with separate supervisory boards consisting entirely of non-executive directors overseeing the activities of the executive board, which only has executive directors responsible for management. But the corporate issues of the previous decade caused a divide in the Anglo-Saxon approach. Company regulators in the United States, at both the federal and state levels, responded to problems of corporate behaviour with new regulation and company law, supported by the rules of the relevant stock exchanges. The United Kingdom and other commonwealth countries, however, preferred to regulate companies through voluntary codes of best practice.

The first corporate governance code was the Cadbury Report (1992)[40] in the United Kingdom, produced by a committee chaired by Sir Adrian Cadbury. The code covered the governance of public listed companies in the United Kingdom. Cadbury declared that 'corporate governance' is the system by which companies are directed and controlled. In essence, the Cadbury Code called for:

---

[37] Mintzberg, Henry (1984) Who should control the corporation? *California Management Review*, October 1, 90–115.

[38] Tricker, R. I. (1984) *Corporate Governance – Practices, Procedures and Powers in British Companies and Their Boards Of Directors*. Gower, London.

[39] Cochran, Philip L. and Wartick, Steven L. (1988) *Corporate Governance: a Review of the Literature*. Financial Executives Research Foundation, Morristown.

[40] The Report of the Committee on *'The Financial Aspects of Corporate Governance.'* Vol. 1, December 1992, Gee, London (The Cadbury Report).

~ the inclusion of independent board members, with independence carefully defined

~ the separation of the roles of chairman of the board from the chief executive officer. If the two roles were combined, then there should be strong independent directors on the board

~ the formation of an audit committee of the board, comprising non-executive directors, to liaise with the independent external auditors and oversee financial matters

~ the use of a remuneration committee of the board with non-executive directors to oversee senior executive remuneration

~ the formation of a nomination committee with non-executive directors to identify and propose new board members for the approval of the board.

Companies did not have to meet the recommendations. Following the Cadbury Code was voluntary, although companies were required to report on their compliance with the Code and, if they had not, to explain why. The Code was incorporated into the listing rules of the London Stock Exchange, so that the ultimate sanction for failure to meet the Code's requirements was the threat of delisting.

Some critics of the Cadbury Report argued that it went too far: 'the emphasis on the importance of non-executive directors introduces the controls over executive management of the European two-tier supervisory board', which was an anathema to many UK directors. On the other hand, others felt that the report did not go far enough: 'failure to follow the Code should have been legally enforceable.'

Sir Adrian Cadbury, however, was always keen to emphasise that his report was about the *financial aspects* of corporate governance, recognising that the subject had behavioural, legal and political aspects. The Cadbury Report was the world's first, but other countries quickly followed that lead, producing their own voluntary Corporate Governance Codes. These included the Viénot Report (1999[41]) from France, the King Report (1994)[42] from South Africa, the Toronto Stock Exchange Day Report (*Where Were the Directors?*) (1994),[43] the Netherlands Peters Report (1997),[44] and a report on corporate governance from the Hong Kong Society of Accountants (1995 and 1997)[45] that was subsequently included in the Hong Kong Stock Exchange listing rules. As with the Cadbury Report (1992), these reports called for independent oversight

---

[41] https://ecgi.global/sites/default/files//codes/documents/vienot2_en.pdf [42] www.iodsa.co.za/

[43] https://search.library.utoronto.ca/details?1375232

[44] https://ecgi.global/code/peters-report-recommendations-corporate-governance-netherlands

[45] www.hkicpa.org.hk/en/About-us/Advocacy-and-representation/Best-practice-guidance/Publications

of top executive management to prevent abuse of power over a corporation, calling for audit committees, the wider use of genuinely independent outside directors, and the separation of the roles of chairman of the board from CEO to avoid executive domination of decision-making and to protect the rights of shareholders, particularly minority shareholders.

In Australia, a Committee on Corporate Governance (1993) was formed, chaired by Professor Fred Hilmer. Their report added a further perspective to the conformance and compliance emphasis in the Cadbury Code: governance is about performance as well as conformance:

> The board's key role is to ensure that corporate management is continuously and effectively striving for above-average performance, taking account of risk ... this is not to deny the board's additional role with respect to share-holder protection.

Hilmer titled his report *Strictly Boardroom*,[46] a reference to a film popular at the time: *Strictly Ballroom*. The film portrays the world of competitive ballroom dancing, in which originality, innovation and performance had been sacrificed to inflexible and inhibiting rules and regulations. This was the danger facing current governance practices, argued Hilmer, if conformance and compliance overshadowed performance. The author of this Element held a visiting profes-sorship at the Australian Graduate School of Management in 1989 and worked with Hilmer, who added an important extra dimension to Tricker's original quadrant describing a board's duties (see Figure 1).[47] The original simple 2x2 matrix showed boards' 'performance roles' (strategy formulation and policy making) on the right with the 'conformance roles' (executive supervision and accountability) on the left. Hilmer added a central box emphasising that all boards had to work with and through executive management, although the scale of that involvement would vary.

In 1994, the Institute of Directors in South Africa published a corporate governance report by a committee chaired by former Supreme Court judge Mervyn King. Influenced by UK practice, King proposed non-mandatory report-ing of compliance with a code or exploring the reason if not. King was to produce three more corporate governance reports that were increasingly innovative.

In 1998, the Organisation for Economic Co-operation and Development (OECD) published a set of guidelines[48] on corporate governance, encouraging

---

[46] Hilmer, Frederick G. (1993) *Strictly Boardroom – Improving Governance to Enhance Business Performance.* Business Library https://librariesaustralia.nla.gov.au

[47] Tricker, Bob (2019) *Corporate Governance – Principles, Policies, and Practices, 4th ed.* Oxford University Press, Oxford.

[48] Organisation for Economic Co-operation and Development (1999) *OECD Principles of Corporate Governance.* OECD, Paris, France.

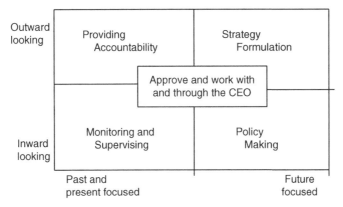

Figure 1 The Work of the Board

governments to adopt them. Their report contrasted the strong corporate governance practices in the United States and Britain with those in Japan, France and Germany, noting that other constituencies, including employees, have a part to play. Some commentators dismissed the OECD proposals as 'pointless'; others saw merit in establishing some core principles of good corporate governance.

In October 1999, the Commonwealth[49] Business Forum resolved that:

> all Commonwealth countries [should] create or reinforce institutions to promote best practice in corporate governance; in particular, codes of good practice establishing standards of behaviour in the public and private sectors should be agreed to secure greater transparency, and to reduce corruption.

The Commonwealth Association for Corporate Governance then published a code of corporate governance principles.[50]

By contrast, corporate governance in the United States is based on compliance with regulation and law,[51] not the discretionary 'comply or explain' approach of the Cadbury and similar corporate governance code. However, in 1997 the United States Business Roundtable, which takes a pro-business perspective, produced a Statement on Corporate Governance, which was updated in 2002. The Statement offered 'guiding principles of sound corporate governance' and stated that: 'The paramount duty of the board of directors of a public corporation is to select a chief executive officer and to oversee this CEO and other senior management in the competent and ethical operation of the corporation on a day-to-day basis.'

---

[49] The British Commonwealth of Nations.

[50] Commonwealth Association for Corporate Governance (November, 1999) *CACG Guidelines: Principles for Corporate Governance in the* Commonwealth. CACG, New Zealand.

[51] This was reinforced, post-Enron, by the 2002 Sarbanes-Oxley Act.

The Statement also suggested that:

~ The responsibility of the board and its audit committee is to engage an independent accounting firm to audit the financial statements prepared by management and to issue an opinion on those statements based on Generally Accepted Accounting Principles (GAAP).
~ The responsibility of the independent accounting firm is to ensure that it is in fact independent, is without conflicts of interest, employs highly competent staff, and carries out its work in accordance with generally accepted auditing standards (GAAS).
~ The responsibility of management is to operate the corporation in an effective and ethical manner in order to produce value for stockholders.
~ The responsibility of management, under the oversight of the board and its audit committee is to produce financial statements that fairly present the financial condition and results of operations of the corporation.
~ The corporation has a responsibility to deal with its employees in a fair and equitable manner.

The proxy votes of institutional investors, cast on behalf of their investors or policyholders, have also influenced corporate governance development. Advisory organisations to the financial sector, study and make recommendations on voting responses to company resolutions at shareholder meetings. In the process, corporate governance can be enhanced. The United States-based Institutional Shareholder Services[52] (ISS) provides such advisory services to their clients in financial institutions. Some clients instruct ISS to handle their proxy voting. In the United Kingdom, the Association of British Insurers[53] and the Pensions and Lifetime Savings Association[54] also advise their members on proxy voting issues.

The California Public Employees' Retirement System has been active in corporate governance development, producing corporate governance principles with benchmarks for practices in the companies in its global portfolio. In response, some companies, such as General Motors, publish their own board governance guidelines.[55]

The environment in which these corporate governance developments were occurring also saw significant changes in organisations being governed. Dynamic, flexible corporate structures, often global, were replacing the more stable, often regional, corporate groups of earlier years. Corporate networks operated across many countries, cultures, time zones, jurisdictions and

---

[52] www.issgovernance.com/about/about-iss   [53] www.abi.org.uk/about-the-abi/about-us
[54] www.plsa.co.uk
[55] https://investor.gm.com/static-files/c09a27f3-a30b-4f88-8888-dd7282766949

currencies. Such groups might form complex networks of subsidiary compan-ies, associated companies and joint ventures. They may also have strategic alliances with crossholdings of shares, cross-directorships, chains of leveraged funding and complex supply chains. The governance, in other words the exer-cise of power over such situations, raised new challenges. In some cases, while claiming to be pursuing shareholders' interests, some directors were seen to be pursuing their own agendas and receiving massive rewards; privileges enjoyed in earlier generations only by monarchs, their courtiers and property-owning aristocrats.

At the end of the 1990s, James D. Wolfensohn, President of the World Bank, suggested that: 'The proper governance of companies will become as crucial to the world economy as the proper governing of countries.'

4 Crisis and Reform in Corporate Governance in the Twenty-first Century

The First Decade of the Twenty-first Century – Enron, Sarbanes–Oxley, Global Crisis

Throughout the twentieth century, the dominant focus of business was on management: management consultants, management theories and management gurus all flourished. Organisation theories were created, although the board of directors seldom appeared on company organisation charts. Strategic planning, financial management and marketing, all developed but with little concern for the role of the directors. This was the era of technocratic management. However, as the twenty-first century dawned, the spotlight had swung to corporate governance. Around the world, the value of sound corporate govern-ance was recognised to promote shareholder interests and enhance share value. Codes or principles or best corporate governance practice covered companies listed on most stock markets. Many of these codes now called for director appraisal, training and development and for board-level performance reviews.

The United States had been developing corporate regulation through the Securities and Exchange Commission (SEC) for many years and US public companies seemed well governed. Some thought that other countries would gradually converge with the successful US corporate governance regime.

Then Enron, one of the largest companies in the United States, failed. Yet the company seemed to have met all the demands of SEC regulation and stock exchange listing rules. It had prestigious, experienced independent directors, all the requisite board committees, and had even separated the roles of board chair and CEO, unlike some other major US corporations. However, subsequent investigations showed that top management had shifted the corporate strategy beyond the supply of energy to trading in energy futures. For a while this delivered good results. But the board had failed to realise that the new strategy had changed the company's risk profile from a relatively low-risk energy supplier to a high-risk financial institution. The Finance Director had also created some 'special purpose vehicles', entities used to raise the highly geared capital needed for the futures business. Finance market conditions changed, and Enron collapsed. Shareholders lost their capital and some executives went to jail for fraud. Enron's auditor, Arthur Andersen, one of the big five international accounting firms, collapsed as clients changed auditors and partners joined other firms. The 'big five' had become the 'big four'.

The United States was not alone in facing companies with governance problems: in the United Kingdom, Marconi, British Rail, Independent Insurance and the Tomkins organisation; in Australia, HIH Insurance; in Italy, Parmalat; and in Germany, Vodaphone Mannesmann, all had governance issues. The company regulatory authorities launched inquiries in each case. Other US public companies – Waste Management, Worldcom and Tyco – also collapsed following corporate governance problems.

The response of the US authorities was further federal law: the 2002 Sarbanes–Oxley Act.[56] Soon dubbed 'Sox' or 'Sarbox', the act was designed to give more protection to shareholders of public listed companies. Only independent directors could now serve on audit and remuneration committees, shareholders had to approve plans for directors' stock options, and subsidised loans to directors were forbidden. Section 404[57] of SOX required companies to publish information in their annual reports on the scope, adequacy and effect-iveness of internal controls including financial control. Sarbanes–Oxley signifi-cantly increased the requirements for corporate governance in the United States and, inevitably, the cost. In the process, the names of Senator Sarbanes and Congressman Oxley became enshrined in the corporate governance lexicon.

A new institution, the Public Company Auditing Oversight Board[58] (PCAOB) was created to oversee audit firms. Auditors of public companies were now required to rotate their audit partners to prevent an over-familiarity between the auditor and the client's finance department. Audit staff must now observe a 'cooling-off period' before joining the staff of an audit client.

Given corporate governance, regulated by company law and SEC require-ments, there was little interest in the United States for the voluntary corporate governance codes that had been introduced by the UK's Cadbury Report and quickly adopted by other countries around the world. However, the National

---

[56] www.sec.gov/answers/about-lawsshtml.html   [57] www.soxlaw.com/s404.htm
[58] https://pcaobus.org/

Association of Corporate Directors (NACD) did produce a report on director professionalism.[59] The Commission's recommendations suggested that key board committees should be composed entirely of independent directors, have a written charter describing their duties and should be able to appoint independent advisors. If the board chairman was not an independent director, the board should appoint an independent director to lead the outside directors, who should hold periodic sessions without the executive directors being present. Audit committees should meet independently with both the internal and independent auditors. Boards should provide new directors with an orientation programme to familiarise them with their company's business, industry trends and governance practices. The American Law Institute published a set of general principles on corporate governance,[60] which generated a debate on the regulation of boards and directors by the courts. Then in 2003, the SEC approved new listing requirements reflecting many of the NACD recommendations.

During the early years of this decade, interest rates in Europe and the United States were low, financial markets were highly liquid, and monetary policies were lax. As a result, loans on property soared and house prices rose, encouraging more borrowing for property purchases. Personal borrowing soared; some on extended credit card debt, others by loans secured on inflated house prices. Loans were made to owners with poor credit ratings. But lenders reduced their exposure to risk by bundling their loan assets into securities, which they then traded with other financial institutions around the world, a process known as securitisation of the sub-prime market. But this bubble was about to burst. House prices began to fall, leaving some owners in negative equity, their debt greater than the value of their property. Banks foreclosed to recover their debts, driving house prices down further.

The financial instruments used to trade the securitised debt were sophisticated. Matching the security with specific mortgages was difficult. It seemed that the outside directors of some banks failed to appreciate the extent of their bank's exposure to risk. Confidence fell as rumours spread of some bank's exposure to dubious sub-prime debt, lowering confidence further. It was suggested that some banks might not be able to meet their obligations, should depositors want to withdraw their funds. Central banks made special arrangements to provide funds to sustain some banks.

In 2007, Bear Stearns, a major financial institution, was bailed out by the US government. Next, Fannie Mae and Freddie Mac, the two US mortgage

---

[59] *Report of the NACD Blue Ribbon Commission on Director Professionalism* (2002). The National Association of Corporate Directors, Washington, DC.

[60] https://quizlet.com/103545286/american-law-institute-principles-of-corporate-governance-flash-cards/

organisations that provide most loans to homeowners in the United States, were given government guarantees of up to US$5 trillion to shore up the market and prevent panic. Then, American International Group (AIG), the world's biggest insurer and provider of hedging cover to the banking sector, imploded. The US government, fearful of the economic and social consequences if AIG failed, provided a loan facility of US$85 billion, secured on AIG assets. The government took an 80 per cent equity stake in the company.

The next financial institution to face problems was Lehman Brothers in New York. But they were not so fortunate. The Federal Reserve refused to provide support and, after 158 years, Lehman Brothers was liquidated. Market confidence fell further. In September 2008, the Federal Reserve and the US Treasury tried to restore confidence, offering to take on banks' bad debts, including the sub-prime loans with their underlying collateral security. Commentators complained that this scheme allowed bankers, whose investment decisions had caused the crisis, to unload all the risky loans at no personal cost, paid for by the taxpayer.

Banks in other countries also faced similar liquidity problems. In 2007, there was a run on a British bank, the first for more than a hundred years. The Northern Rock Bank failed and was taken over by the British government. The Bank of East Asia in Hong Kong faced a run in 2008, which was quickly met by reassurances from Hong Kong's financial authorities. In October 2008, all the banks and the stock exchange in Iceland had to be closed. Iceland, a country of around 300,000 people dependent on fishing and tourism, had been led by a handful of financial entrepreneurs to engage in international finance way beyond the country's economic potential. Given the global financial crisis, the country could not meet depositors' demands. The Icelandic currency became unacceptable and the government appealed to the International Monetary Fund for help.

In the United States, the government invested US$700 billion buying equity shares in US banks. In the United Kingdom, the government effectively nationalised three banks: the Royal Bank of Scotland; HBOS; and Lloyds TSB. In both countries shareholder power and wealth had been eroded.

The global financial crisis raised some fundamental corporate governance issues, including exposure to risk. Independent outside directors were supposed to monitor management. Yet in the failed financial institutions, many directors seemed unaware of the exposure to strategic risk involved in the sophisticated securitised instruments their banks were using. Had large bonuses and share options to executive directors encouraged unacceptable risk-taking? Independent auditors had approved the banks' financial reports without exposing the potential risk. Credit agencies had awarded high credit ratings to companies that, in fact, were exposed to financial catastrophe. The financial regulators also failed to appreciate the financial chaos that was developing.

In response to the catastrophic failure of the financial system, the US government enacted the Dodd–Frank Wall Street Reform and Consumer Protection Act[61] in July 2010; a comprehensive and demanding regulation of the financial sector, demanding higher accountability and transparency. The Securities and Exchange Commission called for all public companies to create board-level committees to consider their companies' exposure to risk. The SEC also called for shareholder votes on top-executive remuneration (although the outcome would be advisory rather than binding), and for the annual election of directors, rather than the staggered, periodic re-election required in many companies' articles. The separation of the role of board chair from chief executive, as required in many corporate governance codes elsewhere, was discussed, but not enforced.

In the United Kingdom, the Financial Review Council proposed changes to the UK corporate governance code to improve the ability for shareholders to ensure that boards were well structured, and to improve boards' effectiveness. Boards' responsibility for corporate risk strategy was emphasised.

Meanwhile, the South African Institute of Directors published two further corporate governance reports, known as King II (2002) and King III (2009), which updated King I (1994). However, the most important South African corporate governance report, King IV (2016),[62] came in the next decade.

The Second Decade of the Twenty-first Century – Corporate Social Responsibility (CSR), Ethics, Diversity, Director Rewards

The OECD had published a set of corporate governance principles designed to help countries develop their own corporate governance codes. Originally published in 2004, the global financial crisis caused these principles to be reviewed.[63] The OECD was joined in 2015 by the G20 group of nations[64] to promote the revised principles.

---

[61] Dodd–Frank Wall Street Reform and Consumer Protection Act [Public Law 111–203] [As Amended Through P.L. 115–174, Enacted May 24, 2018].

[62] www.iodsa.co.za/page/KingIVReport

[63] Kirkpatrick, Grant (2009) *The Corporate Governance Lessons from the Financial Crisis.* February. Also, *Corporate Governance and the Financial Crisis: Key Findings and Main Messages.* June 2009. Both publications available at: www.oecd.org

[64] The updated principles were launched at the meeting of G20 Finance Ministers and Central Bank Governors in Ankara on 4–5 September 2015. They were subsequently endorsed at the G20 Leaders Summit in Antalya on 15–16 November 2015. www.oecd.org/daf/ca/principles-corporate-governance.htm

In 2016, the UK government implemented the European Union Directive on disclosure of non-financial information and diversity statistics.[65] These reporting regulations applied only to large companies. Also, in 2010, the UK Davies Review[66] called for an increase in the number of women in leadership positions of FTSE 350 companies, setting a target of 33 per cent women on their boards by 2020.

The UK Corporate Governance Code,[67] was updated in 2018, reflecting the emphasis of the Companies Act 2006 on relationships between companies, shareholders and other stakeholders. It called for companies to create a corporate culture aligned with the company strategy, promoting integrity and valuing diversity. The code called for board engagement with the workforce to understand their views; to describe how the board has considered the interests of stakeholders.[68] Through the Code, the Financial Reporting Council (FRC) called for boards to have the 'right mix of skills and experience, constructive challenge, and to promote diversity', and the need to 'refresh boards and undertake succession planning', widening the role of the nomination committee to create 'a diverse board'. Some felt that this was an attempt at social engineering by the FRC, arguing that ability to contribute to corporate performance was more important than representative diversity.[69]

Other changes proposed included the reporting of companies' business models and financial strategy; establishing principles on board's responsibility for risk policies; annual re-election of the board chair, with an emphasis on the chair's leadership role; a focus on the roles, skills and independence of non-executive directors; externally facilitated board evaluation reviews at least every three years; regular reviews by the board chair of each director's performance and time availability; and a requirement that if a director's remuneration is related to performance, it should be in line with the company's long-term strategy and risk profile.

In 2016, the Institute of Directors in South Africa published King IV[70] Corporate Governance Report, which has been called a 'ground-breaking' contribution. The report emphasised the ethical and societal responsibilities of governing bodies, proposing a board social and ethics committee. King recognised that all corporate entities need to be governed, and his report is applicable

---

[65] https://eur-lex.europa.eu/legal-content/EN/TXT/?uri=CELEX%3A32014L0095

[66] www.gov.uk/government/news/lord-davies-ftse-350-boards-should-be-33-female-by-2020

[67] *Proposed Reforms to the UK Corporate Governance Code* (2009) FRC PN 287, 1 December. Available at: www.frc.org.uk/getattachment/31de1771-1020-4568-9b22-ab95796a1da5/2009-Review-of-the-Combined-Code-Final-Report1.pdf

[68] UK Companies Act 2006, section 172.

[69] www.bobtricker.co.uk Blog 'Boards need ability not diversity', posted 17 October 2017.

[70] https://cdn.ymaws.com/www.iodsa.co.za/resource/collection/684B68A7-B768-465C-8214-E3A007F15A5A/IoDSA_King_IV_Report_-_WebVersion.pdf

to them all – private and public sectors, profit and not-for-profit organisations. Compliance remained voluntary, although the Johannesburg Stock Exchange made compliance a listing requirement.

Yet, as the second decade of the twenty-first century drew to a close, many issues affecting the way power was exercised over corporate entities remained unresolved around the world.

5 The Frontiers of Corporate Governance

Some issues on the frontiers of corporate governance raise fundamental matters of principle, which have yet to be considered in depth. Other unresolved issues on the frontiers are matters of corporate governance practice.

Unresolved Issues of Principle

The Role of Executive Directors in Corporate Governance

Some years ago, when the boards of major British companies were dominated by executive directors, the Chairman of the Delta Metal Company commented that 'the problem with executive directors is that they are marking their own examination papers'. This apparent problem has been addressed in both the United Kingdom and the United States by requiring boards of major companies to have a majority of genuinely independent outside (non-executive) directors. In the two-tier board, of course, the matter does not arise because the executive board is quite separate from the non-executive supervisory board.

Nevertheless, an issue of principle remains for the unitary board: what is the proper role of the executive directors as board members? Is it their duty to be equally responsible with the other directors for the governance of their company, as company law suggests? Or, is it to present the board with the management situation, accepting responsibility for the corporate performance, and answering the independent directors' questions; while the outside directors determine whether the executives' performance is satisfactory?

In many private companies and public companies dominated by their founders or other powerful individuals, the executive directors dominate decision-making, using the independent directors for information and advice. This situation highlights what might be called the performance versus conformance paradox of the unitary board, which is responsible for both setting the overall strategic direction of the enterprise and delivering long-term performance, whilst ensuring conformance to the policies and plans the board has made and ensuring it meets the demands of shareholders and regulatory authorities. In other words, the unitary board is expected to be involved in strategy formulation and policy making, as well as supervising management performance and ensuring accountability.

Most corporate governance codes specify the minimum percentage of independent directors required on the board, and on the audit, nomination and remuneration board committees. The structure and membership of the board, obviously, directly influences board culture, as does the leadership style of the board chair.

The 'Ignorance of Independence' Paradox

A basic tenet of modern corporate governance is the importance given to the independent outside (non-executive) director. Independence is precisely defined in the codes to ensure that these directors have no interest in the company that might, or might be seen to, adversely affect genuine independent and objective judgement. Essentially, to be independent a director should have no interest in the company other than the directorship and, perhaps, an insignificant shareholding. Typically, codes require an independent director not to be or have been previously an employee of the company, not to be a nominee for a shareholder nor a supplier of finance, and not a representative of companies in the up-stream or down-stream added value chains. Close family relationship with a senior executive of the company can also invalidate the claim of independence. Of course, such people may have an important role to play as directors but are then seen as connected outside directors not independent. Some corporate governance codes treat a director who otherwise would be independent, but who has served on the board for a long period, as too close to executive management and, therefore, no longer considered independent.

This situation highlights the 'ignorance of independence' paradox: the more independent directors know about a company's business, organisation, strategies, markets, competitors and technologies, the less independent they become; while the greater the ignorance of outside directors about the business, the greater their independence! Yet it is the outside director who really knows the business who can contribute most to strategy formulation, policy making, risk assessment, management succession planning, executive supervision and handling crisis situations. Again, we see the importance of board culture and the significance of the leadership role of the board chair.

Corporate Governance by Statutory or Voluntary Compliance?

In the past, some commentators on corporate governance distinguished what they call the 'Anglo-American' approach (unitary boards with both executive and independent directors) based on common law, from the 'Continental

European' approach (two-tier boards with a non-executive supervisory board supervising the executive board) based on Roman civil law. However, fundamental differences exist between the Anglo and American concepts of corporate governance compliance.

In the United Kingdom and other countries influenced by the development of UK law, including all the countries of the British Commonwealth,[71] corporate governance is based on voluntary adherence to corporate governance codes (follow the code or explain why not). Since these corporate governance codes have typically been written into stock exchange listing rules for quoted companies, compliance is usually ensured.

In the United States, and countries influenced by US law, the governance of companies is determined by legally enforceable regulation, mandated by the Securities and Exchange Commission at the federal level and by state company law (obey the law or face the consequences).

The European Union's attempts to harmonise company law throughout member states, and thus converge corporate governance policies and practices, has not always been successful. An attempt to mandate the German style two-tier board[72] was thwarted by the United Kingdom. Britain's referendum decision to leave the European Union, of course, raised significant company law and corporate governance issues.

In the People's Republic of China, a one-party state, the approach to corporate governance is evolving. This enables the authorities, at the state, provincial and local levels, to control enterprises, encouraging entrepreneurial development and economic growth for 'the good of the people' (i.e. the state).

It is apparent that that the principles, policies and practices of corporate governance hinge on the economic and political orientations, and the cultural inheritance, including the law, of the country in which the corporate entity is incorporated. In other words, corporate governance compliance by the adherence to principle or regulation depends on the cultural, economic and political context.

The Role of Companies in Society

Typically, relationships between corporate entities and the rest of society are defined and protected by law: company law; contract law; employment law; consumer protection law; health and safety law; environmental protection law; and so on. Some recent developments in company law, including in the United

---

[71] Including Australia, Canada, Hong Kong, New Zealand, Newfoundland, South Africa and the Irish Free State.

[72] European Commission (1972) Draft fifth directive on company law harmonisation.

Kingdom,[73] have called for companies to recognise the effect of their actions on other stakeholders; without, however, requiring them to report to or be accountable to them.

Two US corporate lawyers, Blair and Stout,[74] have critiqued the principle of shareholder primacy.

Some recent developments have also questioned the role of companies in society. The United Nations Compact[75] on sustainability and the environment, which has been adopted by over 10,000 companies in more than 150 countries, requires adherence to ten principles on human rights, labour relations, the environment and corruption. The Statement of the Purpose of the Corporation, published by the US Business Roundtable in August 2019,[76] replaces shareholder primacy with a commitment to all stakeholders – customers, employees, suppliers, communities and shareholders. The 'triple bottom line' (TBL) is an accounting framework that reports on the social, environmental and financial performance of an enterprise. Corporate regulators, in some countries, also now require regular reports on companies' environmental impact, sustainability and employee diversity. In January 2020, Microsoft announced an aggressive programme to cut its carbon emissions by more than half within the next ten years, both within the company and its supply chain.

Nevertheless, whilst recognising that companies must satisfy all stakeholders, the goal of many institutional investors, representing vast employee pension funds as well as affluent investors, remains the increase of shareholder wealth through sustainable profit. Some board chairmen and chief executive officers accept that judgement.

Calls for boards of directors to recognise their responsibility for setting their company's moral compass reflects such changing societal concerns. Corporate governance literature tends to treat the place of companies and other corporate entities in society as a given. The values and behaviours expected of key participants are seldom recognised. Such concerns raise fundamental questions about relationships between individuals, corporate entities and states.

---

[73] UK Companies Act 2006, Section 172.

[74] Blair, M. M. and Stout, L. (1999) A team production theory of corporate law. *Virginia Law Review*, 85, 247; Blair, M. M. and Stout, L. (2001a) Director accountability and the mediating role of the corporate board. *Washington University Law Quarterly*, 79, 403; Stout, L. (2012) *The Shareholder Value Myth*. Cornell Law Library https://scholarship.law.cornell.edu/cgi/viewcontent.cgi?article=2311&context=facpub

[75] www.unglobalcompact.org

[76] www.businessroundtable.org/business-roundtable-redefines-the-purpose-of-a-corporation-to-promote-an-economy-that-serves-all-americans

Again, we see that the principles, policies and practices of corporate governance hinge on the cultural, economic and political context of the state in which the entities exist.

The Role of the State in Corporate Governance

Concerns about the rightful place of corporate entities in society highlight the potential significance of the state. The state enacts the law that enables every corporate entity to exist and operate. The law regulates their behaviour.

In the Western world, the cultural tendency is to allow corporate entities freedom to pursue their objectives within laws designed to protect the rest of society. That is not the case in all societies.

In China, now the world's second largest economy, the state's power over corporate entities, both state-owned and privately owned enterprises, is still evolving. Inevitably, in this one-party state, the government's interest is to ensure that all corporate entities act in the interests of the state, what is usually referred to as 'the interests of the people'. In the case of state-owned enterprises, control is maintained through government departments and agencies. Inevitably, there is an ongoing tension between these companies' concern for entrepreneurial, financial and strategic freedom that must be set against the state's need to control its economy, national strategic interests and societal needs. Some Chinese companies are large, listed on stock exchanges in China and, for a few abroad, particularly in the United States, they must satisfy Securities and Exchange Commission (SEC) corporate governance regulations.

China's economic reforms have created an affluent, property owning middle-class (at least in the large cities in the east of the country), although many of them still approach the stock market as they might a casino.

Obviously, state involvement in corporate entities varies considerably between countries. At one end of the scale, free-market minimum corporate regulation is the mode, while at the other end, corporate entities are seen as part of, and therefore controlled by, the state. An understanding of corporate governance in each country calls for an appreciation of that country's cultural inheritance.

Issues of Practice

Nomination and Appointment of Members to Governing Bodies

Some boards of directors and other governing bodies are self-appointed, self-rewarding and self-perpetuating elites. Although the constitutions of most companies, institutions, and other societies provide for members of that organisation to elect their governing body, the reality is that power to nominate often resides within a small group. This may be because the membership is large and diverse. Members may be content with the enterprise's performance and not interested in its governance. Or opportunities may not exist for them to be involved in any meaningful way in the nomination and appointment of directors. The requirement in corporate governance codes for a board-level nomination committee, comprised of independent directors to avoid domination by top management, does not necessarily resolve the problem, because those independent directors on the nomination committee are part of the governance elite.

The issue on the frontier of corporate governance is whether the processes for the nomination and appointment of members of a corporate entity's governing body genuinely enable all members of that body to exercise the rights enshrined in its constitution.

Board Diversity

Calls for board diversity, around the world today, are typically calls for gender diversity, recognising that the boards of many companies have a predominance of men, thus failing to benefit from the contribution women could make. Regulatory authorities have recognised this issue for some years. In some countries, it is a statutory requirement to have a given quota of women on the board; or, in other countries, companies have been exhorted to achieve a given percentage of women on the board by a given date.

The percentage of women on the boards of major companies in many countries has been increasing. Predictably, the proportion of women board members reflects the culture of the country, with companies in Scandinavia having a high percentage, whilst Japan has very few and Saudi Arabia none.

One problem in appointing more women is the apparent lack of women with appropriate senior management experience and strategic-level business knowledge to make them suitable for nomination. In response, some companies have made efforts to break the so-called 'glass ceiling' to enable more women to gain top-management experience.

However, other calls for board diversity include calls for boards to reflect stakeholders, whose interests might be affected by corporate activities. In a limited liability company, for example, these stakeholders might include employees, suppliers, customers and other societal stakeholders. Advocates of such board diversity emphasise the apparent domination of many boards by elderly, white, Anglo-Saxon males and call for boards to represent age, ethnicity and social class. Such proposals emphasise the fundamental question of the role of corporate entities in society.

Succession Planning for the Board Chair

Corporate governance codes require board nomination committees to make recommendations for filling board vacancies. In effect, the nomination committee is responsible for succession planning at board level. However, the chairman of the board is, typically, elected by the directors, not the shareholders. Consequently, the nomination committee is not formally responsible for recommending the appointment to the board chair. Yet the board chair plays a fundamental role in board and corporate leadership, and in creating the board culture. Every board needs to plan for the succession of the board chair. Many do not. Perhaps, the first task of an incoming board chair should be to start the process of finding a successor and, if necessary, set up the necessary training and development programme.

Board Dynamics, Politics and Culture

Corporate governance research has considered the outcomes of board decisions; yet little interest has been shown in the process involved in making them. In other words, the dynamics of board and committee meetings and the interactions between directors outside the boardroom remain largely an unopened black box. Such studies would throw light on board culture and the socio-political interaction between board members. Such insights might also demonstrate that, among other things, corporate governance involves a political process.

John Zinkin, a governance consultant in Malaysia,[77] recently commented that many board members he met had difficulty matching the demands of corporate governance regulations and codes with the reality they face in their own boardroom.

The Protection of Minority Shareholders

Company law, in most jurisdictions, tries to protect the interests of minority shareholders from decisions passed by the majority holding voting power. However, the law cannot protect a minority when a company's constitution allows dual-class or multiple-class shares, which give multiple voting rights to their owners, including company founders, their families and associates. Provided the existence of such potential domination is public knowledge,

---

[77] Writing to me in 2019, with a draft of his latest book: Zinkin, John (2019). *Better Governance Across the Board – Creating Value Through Reputation, People and Processes*. The Alexandra Lajoux Corporate Government Series, De Gruyter.

investors have a choice. So, information about the existence of such voting rights, their ownership and the possible effect becomes important.

In recent years, the founders of many successful high-tech companies hold dual-class shares, giving them voting rights greater than those of outside investors, thus enabling them to maintain control of their enterprise, even though raising significant additional capital for expansion. Typically, stock markets and potential investors accept this situation to their advantage as the companies prosper. However, a question arises on the succession of these founding-fathers: will their dominant voting rights die with them? Or will the privileged voting-right shares pass to others, who lack the justification for that privilege?

Director Information Systems

Information technology and artificial intelligence offer an enormous potential for the future of corporate governance, particularly in enabling directors to receive information and communicate with management and their board colleagues. For many boards, the days of monthly packs of paper reports circulated before each board meeting are already over, with information provided electronically to each director.

Since board-level information systems inevitably contain confidential and externally attractive content (and for listed companies, stock market price-sensitive material), full protection is essential against hacking and other illegal access, erroneous updating and malicious illegal interference. Director-level information systems are among the most sensitive in every organisation.

Developments in systems that enable access to information about the corporate financial, economic, competitive and political environment promise further benefits to directors and their staff. Instant updating, however, has potential drawbacks. A coherent perspective of an entity's strategic situation is not obtained from real-time data. By attempting to keep in touch through frequent access, directors may develop a distorted perspective, be tempted to dabble in day-to-day management activity and waste a lot of their time.

On the frontier of board-level information are artificial intelligence algorithms that provide directors and top management with models of the potential impact of emerging economic, financial, market or political trends affecting the future of their enterprise.

Allegedly Excessive Director Remuneration

Throughout the economically advanced world, concern developed about allegedly excessive levels of director remuneration. Research has shown that the disparity between directors' remuneration and that of the average worker in the same organisation has grown, and continues to grow, from twenty or thirty times to many hundreds of times. Arguments justifying this situation include the shortage of, and competition for experienced, successful top-management talent, increasing world-wide demand, international comparisons and the relatively short duration of many such appointments. Attempts to control board-level remuneration have included more detailed reporting of the nature, duration and amount of each director's remuneration, requirements for shareholder voting on director rewards and calls for the refund of pensions or other rewards based on performance that has not been achieved. Encouragement has also been given to long-term performance-related rewards linked to the growth of a listed company's share price.

International competition could, ultimately, put the brake on runaway top man-agement rewards. The top executives of China's state-owned enterprises are paid on the same scales as other civil servants of similar rank. Clearly, this provides these companies with a significant profit advantage over their international competitors whose executives receive a massively larger slice of corporate profits.

Combining the Roles of Board Chair and Chief Executive Officer

Many corporate governance codes advise against or prohibit power at the top of a company being in the hands of a single person with the responsibilities of Chief Executive Officer or Chair of the Board, sometimes with the added title of President. The corporate governance concern is the domination of a company, which can be avoided by splitting the responsibilities between the CEO and board chair. Yet corporate leadership in the hands of a single person is still the case, particularly in public companies run by their founders, many of them in the United States.

A related issue is whether a CEO should be 'promoted' to the board chair on retiring as executive head. Arguments in favour emphasise the value of the CEO's experience, knowledge and network of contacts. Those against suggest that a retiring CEO who becomes board chair, may have difficulty in releasing day-to-day executive decisions to the successor, interfering in man-agement; whereas the role of chair involves leading the board not managing the company. Some corporate governance codes prohibit the practice.

These issues are likely to remain on the frontier of corporate governance until attitudes or political imperatives change.

Improving the Effectiveness of Boards, Committees and Individual Directors

The requirement in many corporate governance codes for regular performance appraisal of boards, board committees and individual directors has put the improvement of board-level performance on the frontier of governance topics.

Significant differences between the way boards operate, board cultures and board leadership styles have become apparent. The search for the most appropriate in given circumstances is under the spotlight.

The Governance of Strategic Risk

Board-level responsibility for recognising corporate risk was not mentioned in the original Cadbury corporate governance report. However, the subsequent catastrophic and life-changing effects of unforeseen strategic events have been well publicised. Board responsibilities for establishing and monitoring policies that identify and manage risk throughout the organisation are now accepted and, indeed, covered in some corporate governance codes. Most corporate entities recognise risk at the operational and managerial levels, and respond to them through insurance, backup systems and procedures, or accepting that level of risk. Although, the presentation of that information to the board could sometimes be better.

The recognition, assessment and policy decisions on strategic risk, however, remain frontier topics. Failure to recognise strategic risk inherent in the electronic systems on which companies' many businesses increasingly depend – airlines and banking, for example – have already cost some companies not only significant loss of profit, but unquantifiable loss of reputation. The strategic threats of cyber-crime are also being overlooked by some corporate entities.

The Board's Role in Creating a Corporate Ethical Profile

As with risk, Cadbury did not include business ethics as a component of corporate governance. Although, in fairness, he emphasised that his report was just about the financial aspects of corporate governance. Subsequent developments that have already been traced in this Element indicate why corporate ethics,[78] corporate social responsibility, sustainability and other societal issues now appear on the board agenda.[79] Although many directors recognise that board decisions may have ethical implications, the fact that through those decisions the board establishes an ethical profile for their organisation is less widely understood. How to define, establish and maintain such a profile remains a frontier topic.

---

[78] For an in-depth review of the relationship between business ethics and corporate governance see Tricker, Bob and Tricker, Gretchen (2014) *Business Ethics – A Stakeholder, Risk, and Governance Approach*. Routledge, London.

[79] Clarke, Thomas (2016) The widening scope of director's duties: the increasing impact of corporate social and environmental responsibility. *Seattle University Law Review*, 39, 557–602.

The Role of Shareholders in Listed Companies

In the nineteenth-century model of the limited liability company, as we saw earlier, shareholders often attended meetings of their company and had the opportunity, indeed were expected, to take part. In major public companies, today, shareholders tend to be numerous, various and remote, with institutions investing more than retail investors. Nevertheless, calls are being made for investors, particularly those institutional investors, to play a greater role in the governance of the companies in which they invest.

In fact, in the United Kingdom and the United States, investor activism in listed companies has increased in recent years. Corporate reports outlining a company's situation and strategies are now more integrated and fuller. Shareholders are better informed.

Moreover, institutional investors are often advised about their voting options – by shareholder advisory groups – on strategic and other corporate decisions such as director appointments and remuneration. As a result, companies have increased their investor relation activities. In many companies, the investor relations website contains considerable information and may, also, provide an opportunity for investors and other interested parties to seek responses to their questions about the company.

The ability to interact with the company and obtain instant information, from anywhere in the world, will recreate the close relationship that existed between shareholder and company in the early days. Such developments are in their infancy and suggest interesting possibilities.

Transparency Versus Stock Market Protection

There is a downside, however, to increased investor relations and greater shareholder activism. Stock markets are, rightly, insistent that all shareholders have access to identical corporate information at the same time, to protect the integrity of the market. Should one shareholder have access to information, perhaps through direct communication with the company, that shareholder would have an advantage over the rest of the market. Access to corporate information needs to be balanced to in order to protect market integrity. This is a field for further development.

The Independence of External Auditors and Other Board Advisors

In the United States, as we have seen, the Sarbanes–Oxley Act arose from the collapse of Enron and over-familiarity between auditors Arthur Andersen and the Enron finance department. This legislation called for the rotation of audit partners and periodic changes in external auditor. Similar regulations now apply in the United Kingdom and other countries around the world.

The external audit of most international, listed companies is in the hands of just four international accounting firms. These entities are large, competitive businesses, intent on growth and the creation of wealth, offering taxation and other consultancy services in addition to independent audit. Ensuring that the audit function, required under the law, remains independent of other services provided by the accountancy firm continues to be a frontier topic. The creation of so-called 'Chinese Walls' between the consultancy and audit functions requires policing and, some say, greater transparency. The suggestion has been made[80] that the two functions be totally separated by law, with the auditor reporting not to the shareholders, which in reality means to the board, but to company regulators.

Similar calls are sometimes heard for genuine independence between company officers and firms providing consultancy and other advisory services to the board.

Aggressive Tax Avoidance

International companies, quite rightly, continue to manage their tax affairs around the world in keeping with the laws of the countries involved, to maximise the long-term benefit for their shareholders. Inevitably, this means that corporate taxation policies arrange for profits to be declared in tax havens with low or zero tax rates. Predictably, this has raised concerns in countries in which the profits have really been generated through the provision of goods or services. Indeed, companies including Amazon, Apple and Starbucks have faced customer resistance because of these perceptions.

Effective changes in taxation policies can only be achieved by international agreement, which would not be in the interests of tax havens in which the profits are currently being declared. It also raises a related issue: many tax havens are in the overall protection of the British Crown.

The Changing Context of Corporate Governance

The final frontier on which corporate governance now stands recognises that new forms of corporate entity will emerge, new sources of capital[81] replace existing capital markets, and new corporate governance principles, policies and practices will be created. Corporate governance principles, policies and practices will need to respond.

---

[80] Bob Tricker blog – www.bobtricker.co.uk – and OUP Corporate Governance blog Mallin and Tricker – corporategovernanceoup.wordpress.com.

[81] Including, for example, Bitcom trading platforms, crowdfunding, private equity and sovereign funds.

6 The Relevance of Culture

In recent years, commentators on corporate governance have increasingly emphasised the importance of culture; a word that Sir Adrian Cadbury did not use in his 1992 report. But the more recent commentaries writing about 'culture', fail to explain what they mean by 'culture', turning the word into a convenient cloak on clarity.

Belief systems lie at the core of a culture. A community's belief system determines its values, influences its perceptions and affects the choices that are made, whether that community is a country, a company or a board of directors. That is why culture is a crucial component of corporate governance. The culture influences morals, ethical standards and the behaviour that is considered acceptable.

Every society develops its own unique culture over time. All organisations, including every company, acquire a culture. So do all committees and boards of directors. A culture mirrors the heritage of beliefs, expectations and values shared by people in that community. Cultures are multi-faceted: history, tradition, religion, language and leadership can all be influential, as can legal, political, social and economic factors. Religious beliefs (or the lack of them) affect personal values, relationships and attitudes to authority in every society. Underpinning beliefs are reflected in the way business decisions are made, organisations run and corporate governance practices develop. They vary in different countries, communities and companies. Culture reflects the ethical context and the moral influence in creating law, doing business and developing corporate governance practices.

The culture of a country, a company or a committee influences what is thought of as important, acceptable, right or wrong. It affects how people think and behave. For organisations, culture mirrors 'the way things are done here'. Often nebulous and opaque, culture can accelerate, reinforce or slow down change.

An appreciation of the relevance of culture is fundamental to an understanding of corporate governance. Much of the thinking, research and writing of the subject, in recent years, has focused on countries that share Anglo-American beliefs in representative democracy, personal freedoms and inalienable rights of the individual, supported by the rule of law through a judiciary independent of the state, and the existence of accountable, democratic institutions. Such orientations affect the governance of corporate entities under that culture.

But they are not shared in other countries, which are now significant in the global economy. Different cultures can produce different corporate governance policies and practices.[82]

---

[82] In this Element it is obviously not feasible to provide detailed comparative descriptions of corporate governance practices around the world. For more information see:

In **Germany**, a commitment to representative democracy has been extended to embrace 'co-determination'. The two-tier board model, with executive directors forming an executive board overseen by a supervisory board of non-executive directors, representing capital and labour, protects the interests of shareholders and employees. Germany's co-determination laws view companies, essentially, as a partnership between labour and capital. This foundation of 'co-determination', can be traced back more than 500 years to the teaching of Martin Luther,[83] who did much to shape that country, its language and the role of the state in its culture (rather than the church). Northern European nations were also influenced by the teaching of John Calvin, who emphasised the importance of working for the benefit of the community, not just oneself and family.

In **Japan**, the *keiretsu* model governs networks connecting groups of Japanese companies through cross holding of shares and interlocking directorships. Social cohesion is a dominant feature of Japanese life, influenced over the years by the Shinto and Buddhist religions. In companies, high levels of unity exist throughout the organisation, with non-adversarial relationships, lifetime employment, personnel policies emphasising commitment, enterprise unions, initiation into the corporate family, cross-functional training, and promotion based on loyalty and social compatibility.

The board of the central company in the *keiretsu* network tended to be very large, comprising the upper echelons of management, with close informal relationships between the members. The concept of independent non-executive directors was not welcomed because it was felt that such people would not understand the business or its culture, while the executive directors had devoted their working lives to the company. Meetings of the entire board tended to be formal, sometimes ceremonial, and were decision-ratifying rather than Western-style decision-making bodies. This reflected the Japanese *ringi* approach to decisions, in which many levels of management participate, developing alternatives, until a clear consensus is reached. The chairmen and senior directors of companies in the *keiretsu* meet regularly and have close, informal relationships.

However, the poor performance of Japan's economy in recent years has led to suggestions from the OECD and some overseas institutional investors for

---

Tricker, Bob and Li, Gregg (2019) *Understanding Corporate Governance in China.* Hong Kong University Press, Hong Kong.

Tricker, Bob (2019) *Corporate Governance – Principles, Policies, and Practices, 4th ed.* Oxford University Press, Oxford.

[83] Schwartz, Robert (1986) *Martin Luther – An Introduction to His Life and Work.* Fortress Press, Minneapolis.

independent directors to be appointed to *keiretsu* boards to challenge the existing complacent paternalistic patterns of governance. Prime Minister Sninzo Abe's call for such outside directors was strongly resisted by many directors, until it was mandated in company law.

In **South Korea**, the *chaebol* conglomerate groups of companies came together following government funding after the Second World War. These *chaebol* groups are connected by family interests both in ownership and board membership. The *chaebol* governance model emphasises a hierarchy of relationships between family members and close associates based on mutual trust and inter-dependence, suggesting influences from Chinese Confucian beliefs.

Over the past thirty years, **China** has grown from a state-owned and dominated economy to become the market-orientated second largest economy in the world. From the outset, China's modernisation programme saw that corporate governance was central to success. Many state-owned enterprises were privatised, some floated on the Chinese stock markets, a few even listed abroad. A new Companies' Act was passed, enabling private companies to be incorporated. State institutions were created to regulate companies.

But China is a one-party state. The judiciary is part of the state apparatus, unlike Anglo-Saxon jurisdictions. Consequently, the courts serve the interests of the state, referred to as 'the people', which means in practice the interests of the Chinese Communist Party. China has created a unique approach to corporate governance, which has adapted some aspects of both the unitary board and supervisory boards, including outside directors on the unitary board, with representatives of the Party on the supervisory board. The driving force of corporate governance with Chinese characteristics has been the creation of wealth, while serving the interests of the people and the state. By contrast, the Anglo-Saxon model of corporate governance is the way companies are regulated and controlled, while exposing unacceptable board-level behaviour. China continues to improvise its way through the evolution of governance – both at the state and the corporate level – responding to the changing needs of this vast population and economy.

The early moral influence in China was Confucianism, founded around 500 BC. This was not a religion with deities, but a teaching calling for respect for others and a sense of continuity based on a hierarchy of authority. Rather than offering a set of moral values, Confucianism called for social harmony, filial respect and relationships based on mutual trust and inter-dependence. In China today, in both personal and business dealings, special relationships and connections, known in Chinese as *guanxi*, are paramount.

Chinese people also play a fundamental part in business life throughout Southeast Asia. Many companies in the major economies – Singapore, Taiwan, Malaysia, Thailand, Indonesia and the Philippines – are in the hands of Chinese families. In the governance of these **overseas Chinese** companies, the board plays a supportive role to the exercise of power by the head of the family, with key management positions held by family members. Some of these companies are diverse groups with considerable delegation of power to the subsidiary units, but with the owner–manager, or a family-orientated small group, exercising control. Should such a company be listed on a stock market, a voting majority is kept in the family. Conceptually, family members feel they have invited these external sharcholders to join the outer circle of the family. Consequently, regulatory authorities emphasise the importance of full disclosure and the control of related-party transactions.

Research[84] into the management and governance of companies owned by overseas Chinese has suggested some distinguishing characteristics about their management and governance. Such firms tend to be:

~ entrepreneurial, often with a dominant entrepreneur, so that decision-making is centralised, with close personal links emphasising trust and control;
~ family-centric with close family control;
~ controlled through an equity stake kept within the family;
~ a paternalistic management style, in a social fabric dependent on relationships, emphasising social harmony, avoiding confrontation and the risk of 'losing face';
~ strategically intuitive, with the business seen as more of a succession of ventures, relying on intuition, superstition and tough-minded bargaining rather than strategic plans, brand-creation or quantitative analysis.

Although **Hong Kong** has been a Special Administrative Region (SAR) of China since 1997, the joint agreement with Britain, which ran the territory previously, allowed Hong Kong to keep its law courts and legal system based on English common law, its existing corporate governance model based on the UK system, with a voluntary corporate governance code, its own currency and tax system and a partially representative democratic Legislative Council, albeit with significant control exercised by mainland China and the subject of considerable recent unrest among Hong Kong residents.

The importance of the cultural context is apparent if corporate governance is to be understood.

---

[84] For more information on the business methods of overseas Chinese, see Redding, S. Gordon (1993) *The Spirit of Chinese Capitalism*. de Gruyter, Berlin; New York.

7 Corporate Governance in Theory

After the Second World War, the dominant focus of organisational research was on management. New management theories and frameworks were developed. Books on management multiplied. Management writers, Ansoff,[85]Drucker,[86] Porter[87] and many others, were published. Management consultants flourished. But the board of directors seldom appeared on the organisation chart. The study of governing bodies, their composition, their activities and their performance, went unnoticed. Their role in confirming corporate objectives and strategies, supervising management activities and being accountable to the organisation's members went unstudied until the final decade of the century, when corporate governance was recognised as a legitimate field for serious academic study.

In 1988, Cochran and Wartick[88] produced an annotated bibliography of the (relatively few) research papers on corporate governance they could find. Although some scholars were sceptical:

> Corporate governance lacks any form of coherence, either empirically, methodologically, or theoretically with only piecemeal attempts to try and understand and explain how the modern corporation is run.[89]

During the following quarter-of-a-century various academic disciplines drove the piton spikes further into the rock to try to secure their claim to be explaining corporate governance. The first issue of the refereed research journal *Corporate Governance – An International Review* (Vol. 1, No. 1) was published in January 1993 and continues to thrive.[90]

Jensen and Meckling (1976)[91] provided the foundations for the agency theoretical studies that were to dominate corporate governance research subsequently. But most of the early studies in the field, before the phrase 'corporate governance' was adopted, tended to be pragmatic; observing and writing descriptively, rather than theoretically. Although, as mentioned previously, research by Berle and Means (1932)[92] had shown the shift of power from

---

[85] Ansoff, H. Igor (1969) *Business Strategy.* Penguin, London.

[86] Drucker, Peter F. (1967) *The Effective Executive.* Harper and Row, New York.

[87] Porter, Michael (1980) *Competitive Strategy.* Free Press, New York.

[88] Cochran, Philip L. and Wartick, Steven L. (1988) *Corporate Governance: a Review of the Literature.* Financial Executives Research Foundation, Morristown.

[89] Pettigrew, Andrew (1992) On studying managerial elites. *Strategic Management Journal*, 13(2), 163–82.

[90] https://onlinelibrary.wiley.com/journal/14678683

[91] Jensen, Michael C. and Meckling, William H. (1976) Theory of the firm: managerial behavior, agency costs and ownership structure. *Journal of Financial Economics*, 3(4, Oct.) 305–60.

[92] Berle, Adolf A. and Means, Gardiner C. (1932) *The Modern Corporation and Private Property.* Macmillan, rev. by Adolf Berle (1967) Columbia University, Harcourt, Brace and World, New York.

shareholders to management in major US corporations. Mace (1971)[93] challenged the conventional wisdom that boards acted as a check on management,
showing that: 'Directors tended to provide advice, and only acted in crisis
situations.'

The 1977 report of the UK's Bullock Committee on Industrial Democracy[94]
included research reports on worker–directors. Tricker (1978)[95] and (1984)[96]
studied the structure of the boards and corporate groups of some British public
companies.

However, as mentioned previously, significant drivers of change in corporate
governance came less from research than from official reports, such as the 1987
US National Commission on Fraudulent Financial Reporting (Treadway), the
1992 UK Cadbury Report, which produced the first corporate governance code,
or the 1988 OECD *Principles of Corporate Governance* .[97]

Companies' regulation and legislation also made significant contributions to
corporate governance practices. The SEC 1972 requirement, that US listed
companies create a board-level audit committee with independent directors,
produced research-based and advisory papers.[98] Major legislation in the United
States and the United Kingdom included the US 2002 Sarbanes–Oxley Act,
which followed the collapse of Enron and their auditors Arthur Andersen; the
significantly revised UK Companies Act (2006); developments in the expectations of the UK corporate governance code; and the 2018 US Dodd–Frank
Wall Street Reform and Consumer Protection Act, which followed the global
financial crisis of the previous decade. Similar major changes in regulation,
company law and corporate governance codes also influenced the development
of corporate governance in other countries.

Various academic disciplines have been applied to the study of corporate
governance: law, economics, politics, sociology, psychology and various deriv-
ations of these basic fields of study. Viewing governing bodies and their
relationships with management, their members and other stakeholders through

---

[93] Mace, Myles L. (1971) *Directors: Myth and Reality.* Division of Research, Graduate School of Business Administration, Harvard University, Boston, MA.

[94] Committee of Inquiry on Industrial Democracy (the Bullock Report)
  Hansard, 23 February 1977, vol. 380 cc179–355.

[95] Tricker, R. I. (1978) *The Independent Director: a Study of the Non-executive Director and of the Audit Committee.* Tolley with Deloitte, Haskins & Sells, London.

[96] Tricker, R. I. (1984) *Corporate Governance – Practices, Procedures and Powers in British Companies and Their Boards of Directors.* Gower, London.

[97] Organisation for Economic Cooperation and Development (1999) *Principles of Corporate Governance.* OECD, Paris, France.

[98] For example, Mautz, R. K. and Neumann, F. L. (1970) The effective corporate audit committee. *Harvard Business Review,* Nov./Dec.
  Mautz, R. K. and Neumann, F. L. (1977) *Corporate Audit Committees: Policies and Practices.* Ernst and Ernst, New York.

the lens of a specific discipline reveals one facet of the subject but leaves other perspectives in darkness.

The study of corporate governance lacks a unifying paradigm. So, scholars tend to relate to the work of others in their own field. Consequently, a review of the development of corporate governance research and theory must, inevitably, reflect these disciplinary boundaries.

Practitioners recognise that knowing what goes on in the boardroom and during interactions between directors is fundamental in understanding corporate governance. But empirical investigation into board activity can be difficult. Boards want to protect confidentiality. Listed companies need to avoid a leak of stock-market price-sensitive information. Internal disagreements between directors need to be kept in the boardroom to prevent unwanted media or market interest. Directors might also be concerned about damaging information leaking out, affecting personal reputations, attracting unwanted media attention or generating lawsuits. From a research perspective, the presence of an outside observer during board discussions might change directors' behaviour, rendering objective observation impossible.

Insights from **Psychology** have been applied to the study of directors' perceptions of their board-level activities. Cognitive maps, produced by repertory grid techniques (Kelly [1955], 1963)[99] can be used to chart a director's mindset. Case studies of strategic decisions have also illuminated some directors' behaviour. But psychological theories have not made a significant impact on corporate governance thinking.

The theory of **Corporate Stewardship** owes its existence to company law, which enabled limited liability companies to be incorporated.[100] Under these laws, the legal duty of company directors is to the shareholders who have appointed them. Directors have a responsibility to the members of the company, not any other interest group that might be affected by the company's actions. In other words, stewardship theory expects boards to be responsible for maximising shareholder value sustainably in the long term. Although some subsequent companies' legislation and updates to corporate governance codes call on directors to act in the best interests of the company, while recognising the interests of other stakeholders.[101]

Stewardship theory takes a positive view of the nature of man: that directors can be trusted to act responsibly with integrity in the interest of others, not

---

[99] Kelly, G. A. ([1955], 1963) *The Psychology of Personal Constructs (A Theory of Personality)*. Norton, New York.

[100] In the United States, the company law of each individual state. In the United Kingdom, the first Companies Act in 1862 (VICT CAP.LXXXIX) and subsequent revisions.

[101] For example, the UK Companies Act 2006 and King IV Corporate Governance Report 92016.

themselves. Obviously, some fail, but that does not invalidate the stewardship concept. The stewardship duty of directors to their members can be applied to all corporate entities. For example, the legislation allowing the incorporation of trades unions, building societies (savings and loan associations) and charities typically gives directors a stewardship duty to the members who have elected them. The underpinning of stewardship theory is law. Company law defines a company, with clear boundaries based on ownership. This enables financial accountancy to produce accounts, within the confines of accepted accounting principles, showing the financial position of the company over time, and enabling independent audit and reporting of the directors' stewardship.

Consistent with the mid-nineteenth-century conception of the limited liability company, power lies with the members, who appoint directors who have a fiduciary duty to act as stewards of the shareholders' interest. Inherent in the concept of the company is the belief that directors can be trusted.

Critics of stewardship theory point out that the de facto situation in modern corporations is quite different from that nineteenth-century model. They emphasise that the idea is naive, except in the case of companies with few shareholders, such as a family business or a subsidiary company in a group. In many listed companies today, ownership is not homogeneous; possibly including pension funds, investment trusts, mutual funds, index-tracking funds, hedge funds and other financial institutions, as well as individual 'retail' shareholders. Moreover, the ownership chain can be complex: an individual investor might use a financial advisor, who places the funds in an investment trust, which in turn seeks to gear its portfolio by spreading its resources across a range of equities, property, commodities and other investment trusts.

Recognising this complexity and the naivety of the original simple shareholder/company model, the theory of **Universal Ownership** offers an alternative model of fiduciary capitalism, which recognises that in liquid markets such as the United States and the United Kingdom, listed companies are often held by a highly diversified set of shareholders, including large concentrations held by a few institutional investors.[102] Exponents of the theory argue that these large institutional investors should be involved in governance matters, taking collective action against failing companies. Critics point out that institutional investors do not have homogeneous investment objectives and may be open to claims for negligence if they take governance action.

The global financial crisis brought calls for greater shareholder empowerment, a return to the original idea of shareholder democracy. Institutional

---

[102] In the United States, the hundred largest financial institutions hold more than 50 per cent of all publicly held equity. In the United Kingdom, there is a similar concentration of ownership.

investors could work together to influence companies with specific proposals and even threaten litigation. Some institutions said that they already met regularly with management. Others disagreed, pointing out that independent non-executive directors were appointed to represent shareholder interests and only the directors had the relevant corporate information. Moreover, investor involvement in governance could result in them receiving insider information; and maybe an inability to trade their shares.

Other critics of stewardship theory have complained that company law, the basis of the theory, is normative: that is, it requires compliance with the rule of law, but it is not predictive, and does not show causal relationships between corporate actions and performance, as a sound theory should. Nevertheless, around the world, stewardship theory, rooted in company law, remains the basis of corporate governance codes, practice and reporting. In stewardship theory, shareholders must trust the directors to be stewards of their investment.

Agency Theory takes a less sanguine view of directors' behaviour. The arrival of the joint-stock limited liability company produced shareholders (the principals) who delegated authority to the directors (their agents). Today the situation has been vastly amplified by the scale, diversity and conflicting objectives of investors and the companies in which they invest. The demands for transparency, reporting, accountability, audit, independent directors and the other requirements of company law and securities legislation, plus the demands of regulators and stock exchange regulations and corporate governance codes are all responses to the agency dilemma.

In agency situations, the parties have asymmetrical access to information. The directors know far more about the corporate situation than the shareholders. **Agency Theory** or **Principal–Agent Theory** as it is sometimes called, looks at corporate governance through the lens of the agency dilemma. The theory perceives the governance relationship as a contract between shareholder (the principal) and director (the agent). Directors, it is argued, seek to maximise their own personal benefit, to take actions that are advantageous to themselves but may be detrimental to the shareholders.

The classical definition of agency theory was given by Jensen and Meckling (1976):[103]

> agency theory involves a contract under which one or more persons (the shareholders) engage other persons (the directors) to perform some service on their behalf which includes delegating some decision-making authority to the agent. If both parties to the relationship are utility maximisers there is good

---

[103] Jensen, Michael C. and Meckling, William H. (1976) Theory of the firm: managerial behavior, agency costs and ownership structure. *Journal of Financial Economics*, 3(4, Oct.), 305–60.

reason to believe the agent will not always act in the best interests of the principal.

Anecdotal evidence of such behaviour is not hard to find.

Research in financial economics continued to look at corporate governance through the agency lens (Fama and Jensen, 1983),[104] studying relationships between companies' performance and their corporate governance practices. Agency theory treats shareholders and company boards as two entities. Consequently, researchers do not need access to the boardroom or to individual directors. Data on the governance structures and the performance of listed companies are published, and readily available. The most frequent theoretical basis of papers published in the refereed journal *Corporate Governance – An International Review* has been agency theory.

Williamson (1975, 1988)[105] suggested that large corporate groups could overcome disadvantages of scale by 'the choice of governance structures' in an approach often called **Transaction Cost Economics**, building on the work of Coase (1937).[106] It was suggested that as large companies grow, they could obtain goods and services at lower prices than in the marketplace: but, there comes a break-even point at which the external market becomes cheaper. Therefore, transaction cost economics focuses on management information and control systems, internal and external audit and the whole panoply of corporate governance mechanisms.

Shleifer and Vishny (1997)[107] provided an overview of the field. Stiles and Taylor (2001)[108] observed that 'both transaction cost economics and agency theories assume that directors and managers are given to self-interest'. However, transaction cost analysis focuses on governance processes, whereas agency theory sees the firm as a set of contracts. Although the focus is different, the research is on the firm and its governance structures not board-level behaviour.

Resource Dependency Theory, on the other hand, takes a strategic view of corporate governance. It sees the governing body as the linchpin between company and the resources it needs. These resources could include, for example, access to equity capital and other sources of finance, knowledge of

---

[104] Fama, Eugene and Jensen, Michael (1983) Separation of ownership and control, *Journal of Law and Economics*, 26(June), 301–25.

[105] Williamson, Oliver E. (1975) *Markets and Hierarchy.* Free Press, New York. Williamson, Oliver E. (1988) The logic of economic organization. *Journal of Law, Economics and Organization*, 4(Spring), 65–93.

[106] Coase, Ronald H. (1937) The Nature of the Firm. *Economica*, 4(Nov.), 386–405.

[107] Shleifer, A. and Vishny, R. (1997) A survey of corporate governance, *Journal of Finance*, 52(2, June), 737–83.

[108] Stiles, P. and Taylor, B. (2001) *Boards at Work: How Directors View Their Roles and Responsibilities.* Oxford University Press, Oxford.

relevant technology, links to potential customers and markets, awareness of competitors, and relationships with business, political and other societal networks. Directors are the node of the network connecting the company to its world. Studies from this perspective show how such relationships reduce uncertainty in decisions. The theory finds its roots in organisation theories, for example Pfeffer (1972).[109]

The theory of **Social Networks** recognises that those involved in corporate governance are often linked through personal networks linking those sharing things in common, such as lifestyle, social standing, class, income, education and professional relationships. Directors serving on the boards of various, non-competing companies can be vital nodes in such networks. On the downside, network relationships could be seen to reduce a director's independence.

Recognising limitations in both the stewardship and the agency theoretical approaches, some researchers have attempted to look at the reality of board activities – Lorsch and McIver (1989),[110] Demb and Neubauer (1992),[111] Monks and Minow (1995),[112] and Monks (2008).[113] Critics of research through the study of cases of corporate governance complain that the evidence is statistically irrelevant, largely anecdotal and can be influenced by prejudice, self-centred reporting or biased insights. The counter argument is that corporate governance involves an inter-personal and political process; and is not a group activity that can be statistically controlled.

Longitudinal studies have provided further insights. Filatotchev and Wright (2005)[114] collected material looking at the evolution of corporate governance practices over the life cycles of enterprises and institutions. Concepts from **political economics** were used by Roe (2003),[115] who studied political and social conflict in companies and the institutions of corporate governance, showing how a nation's political economy interacts with its legal structures and financial markets. Other researchers have adopted a broader political

---

[109] Pfeffer, Jeffrey (1972) Size and composition of corporate boards of directors: the organization and its environment. *Administrative Science Quarterly*, 17, 218.

[110] Lorsch, J. W. and McIver, V. (1989) *Pawns or Potentates: the Reality of America's Corporate Boards*. Harvard Business School Press, Boston, MA.

[111] Demb, Ada and Neubauer, Frederich (1992) *The Corporate Board: Confronting the Paradoxes*. Oxford University Press, New York.

[112] Monks, Robert A. G. and Minow, Nell ([1995] 2011) *Corporate Governance, 4th ed.* Wiley, Chichester.

[113] Monks, Robert A. G. (2008) *Corpocracy: How CEOs and the Business Roundtable Hijacked the World's Greatest Wealth Machine*. Wiley, Hoboken, NJ.

[114] Filatotchev, Igor and Wright, Mike (eds.) (2005) *The Life Cycle of Corporate Governance*. Edward Elgar, Cheltenham, UK and Northampton, MA.

[115] Roe, Mark J. (2003) *Political Determinants of Corporate Governance*, Clarendon Lectures in Management Studies Series. Oxford University Press, Oxford.

economy of comparative institutional development in international corporate governance.[116]

Game theory has also been applied to board-level strategy making. Other researchers interested in the behaviour of directors or their interactions on the board have applied the constructs of sociology and psychology.

The theory of **Class Hegemony** considers the directors' self-image and the impact that has on their behaviour. A group of directors may perceive themselves as an elite group, which leads them to dominate the organisation and its external links. New board and top-executive appointments ensure that the elite is maintained, sustaining the directors' views of themselves.

Class hegemony recognises that directors' self-image can affect board behaviour. These theoretical insights are rooted in the socio-political disciplines, using biographical analysis and case research to produce insights into corporate governance. Essentially, such studies look at corporate governance as an interpersonal, political process.

In recent years, a stakeholder perspective, often called **Stakeholder Theory**, has joined Stewardship Theory and Agency Theory as a contender for the role of the key theoretical perspective on corporate governance. The word 'stakeholder' has been adopted to stand in juxtaposition to 'shareholder', emphasising that a company must meet societal responsibilities, rather than acting solely in the shareholders' interest, as called for in stewardship theory.

Stakeholder Theory perceives corporate governance in terms of the relationships between the corporate entity and any other group in society that might be affected by corporate activities and decisions. This includes those in a contractual relationship with the corporate entity, including employees, customers or clients, partners in the supply chain and providers of finance. 'Stakeholders' also include others who could be affected by the corporate entity, including the local community, which would be affected economically, socially and even politically by corporate action. Similarly, at the state or international levels, issues such as aggressive tax strategies and sustainability, environmental, or similar issues could be involved. Of course, shareholders are also stakeholders in their company, but stakeholder theory focuses on the corporate entity in society.

Advocates of the stakeholder perspective believe that corporate entities owe a duty to all those who might be affected by corporate behaviour. Some go further and call for directors to be accountable to their stakeholders. Such responsible behaviour, the stakeholder advocates argue, should be the price

---

[116] Clarke, Thomas (2017) *International Corporate Governance: a Comparative Approach, 2nd ed.* Routledge, London and New York; Clarke,T., O'Brien, J. and O'Kelley, C. (2019) *The Oxford Handbook of the Corporation.* Oxford University Press, Oxford.

society demands from limited companies for the privilege of limiting share-holders' liability for corporate debt.

Stakeholder ideas raise some basic questions about the place of corporate entities in society. In 1975, the UK Accounting Standards Steering Committee produced a discussion paper, *The Corporate Report*,[117] which recommended that all large economic entities should produce regular accountability reports to all stakeholder groups whose interests might be affected by the decisions of that entity. The political implications of this heroic idea quickly relegated the report to the archives. In the United States, proposals for stakeholder accountability in company law came from consumer advocate Ralph Nader (Nader and Green (1980).[118]

Stakeholder thinking faded during the free market, 'growth and greed' atti-tudes of the 1980s. But in the more environmentally and socially concerned world of the late twentieth and early twenty-first centuries, corporate social responsibility and sustainability reporting were taken seriously again. The Royal Society of Arts in England published a report in 1999, titled *Tomorrow's Company*,[119] which advocated wider recognition of corporate responsibility to stakeholders. Turnbull (1997)[120] suggested a systems approach to the identification of relevant stakeholders, citing growing demands for better consumer, environmental and societal protection.

The difficulty for boards attempting to adopt a stakeholder approach is that they no longer have a single constituency (the shareholders) to satisfy nor a single objective (long-term profitability). Moreover, the interests of stake-holder groups potentially conflict, so satisfying them all is not feasible.

In 1998 in the United Kingdom, the Hampel Committee[121] refining the UK corporate governance code, dismissed stakeholder notions, saying 'directors are responsible for relations with stakeholders, but are accountable to the share-holders'. This opinion was well received in British boardrooms, and indeed in boardrooms around the world.

As we saw when discussing stewardship theory, company law typically requires directors 'to act in the way they consider, in good faith, would be

---

[117] www.icaew.com/library/subject-gateways/corporate-reporting/the-corporate-report

[118] Nader, Ralph, Green, Mark and Seligman, Joel (1976) *Taming The Giant Corporation*. W.W. Norton Co., Inc., New York.

[119] www.blueprintforbusiness.org/principles-and-framework/
Clarke, Thomas and Monkhouse, Elaine (1994) *Rethinking the Company*. Financial Times-Pitman, London.

[120] Turnbull, Shann (1997) Stakeholder governance: a cybernetic and property rights analysis in corporate governance. *Corporate Governance: An International Review*, 5(1, Jan.), 11–23; also in Tricker, R. I. (ed.) (2000) *Corporate Governance* – The History of Management Thought series. Ashgate Publishing, London.

[121] www.icaew.com/technical/corporate-governance/codes-and-reports/hampel-report

most likely to promote the success of the company for the benefit of its members [shareholders] as a whole'. However, the UK Companies Act 2006 (section 172) confirmed that duty, but added a set of issues directors must consider in their strategic decisions, including:

~ the interests of the company's employees;
~ the need to foster the company's business relationships with suppliers customers and others;
~ the impact of the company's operations on the community and the environment;
~ the desirability of the company maintaining a reputation for high standards of business conduct.

This legal requirement was controversial, and the courts have yet to rule on its interpretation in practice. However, stakeholder theory received a boost from an unlikely quarter when in 2019 the US Business Roundtable, which represents the leading corporations of America, suddenly abandoned its decades-long commitment to shareholder primacy, with a commitment to serving the interests of all stakeholders in the business enterprise.[122]

Enlightened shareholder theory recognises that stakeholders need to be satisfied for the creation of long-term shareholder wealth. The theory recognises that companies generate profits only by satisfying stakeholder needs and recognising their interests. Dissatisfied contractual stakeholders have a direct effect on corporate performance. Failure to meet societal expectations leads non-contractual stakeholders to react adversely. This theory is grounded in shareholder primacy but differs from classical stewardship theory because boards are required to take stakeholder interests into account.

Inevitably, choices must be made in any attempt to sketch the evolution of theoretical developments in corporate governance. Others will undoubtedly identify other research that has made groundbreaking contributions. But, hopefully, an indication has been given of the main array of lenses that have been used to look at the subject.

Searching for an integrating theory, some commentators speak of the need for a **multi-disciplinary approach**. The problem with multidisciplinary studies is that they can, all too easily, have no academic discipline at all. This raises the question of whether a meta-theory might be possible in a way that enabled the relationships between different theories, not to be integrated, but inter-related to show their focus on corporate governance phenomena.

---

[122] Business Roundtable (2019) *Statement on the Purpose of a Corporation*. Business Roundtable, Washington, DC. https://opportunity.businessroundtable.org/wp-content/uploads/2019/08/BRT-Statement-on-the-Purpose-of-a-Corporation-with-Signatures.pdf

8 A Subject in Search of its Paradigm

Both agency theory and stewardship theory focus at the level of the corporate entity itself, considering relationships between the entity's governing body and its members. Stakeholder perspectives have much wider boundaries, embracing the corporate entity in its societal context. The behaviour of individual players in corporate governance activities, their personal mind-sets and motivations, personalities and foibles, political skills and prejudices do not appear in either the agency or stewardship paradigms: that is the focus of psychological studies.

Sociological perspectives, such as class hegemony theory, focus on a group of directors – a board or a committee.

Each of these theoretical approaches has produced useful insights, but the view of each is partial, providing users with valuable information, provided they understand the level and boundaries of the relevant theory. In other words, each theoretical spotlight illuminates part of the stage but leaves the rest of the action in shadow.

The predominant focus of the early studies of corporate governance was on the mechanics, processes and outcomes of the governance of listed, public companies. The corporate governance codes addressed the structure of boards, proposed roles for board committees, and emphasised the importance of independent non-executive directors.

In the stewardship model, ownership is the basis of power over the company, increasing shareholder wealth, measured by profit, the long-term objective. The principles of company law and financial accounting provided the theoretical underpinning. The agency model accepts the basic structure and role of the corporate entity under the law but questioned whether directors can really be trusted to act as disinterested stewards of shareholder interests.

Subsequently, it became obvious that *all* corporate entities need to be governed, not just public companies. The governance of private companies, charities and other not-for-profit organisations, health authorities, trade unions, educational bodies, professional institutions, and societies in the arts and sciences – all need governance. However, unlike companies, most not-for-profit entities have multiple goals and many stakeholder groups, sometimes with conflicting expectations.

A more complete understanding of corporate governance would need an overview, a meta-theory of corporate governance; a way to link the various theoretical perspectives, covering all forms of corporate entity, to give a more complete and coherent view of reality.

In methodological terms, the 'processual' approach suggested by Pettigrew (1979, 1997)[123] and Langley (1999, 2007)[124] might be useful. Langley (2007) argued that theory is developed from an understanding of how situations come to be constituted, reproduced and adapted as ongoing processes. As Pettigrew (1997) explained the approach: the exploration of the dynamics of 'human conduct and organisational life occur over time at various layers of context ... '

Systems theory may provide a way to appreciate and explore these 'various layers'. A system is a way of perceiving and describing sets of parts and/or procedures that work together to achieve an outcome: 'a country's railway system'; or 'the budgetary control system', for example. Systems provide a convenient way to view and map complex reality. To define a system, its boundary, level, purpose or function and structure need to be determined.

Defining a system's boundary determines what is within the system and what is in that system's environment. The system boundary defines the system's inputs and outputs, thereby indicating its purpose or function. The structure of a system describes its internal components and how they interact.

A system's level defines the detail with which the components and processes of the system are described. One system may have component sub-systems, which themselves could be viewed as separate systems. An analogy frequently used to illustrate system levels describes a helicopter pilot's view as the plane takes off. On the ground, the pilot can see the field or deck in considerable detail, but the field of vision is limited. As the helicopter rises the pilot's horizon broadens, more and more can be seen but in less and less detail.

A systems approach can be applied to the theoretical insights into corporate governance. The various theories, despite their apparent disparity, can each be shown to be focusing on corporate governance phenomena at different system levels and, thus, with different boundaries. Each of the theories previously described can be shown to be at one or other of six different levels:

Level 1 is the level of the individual member of a governing body – the company officer, director or member of any governing body, such as the council members of a professional body, the committee members of a charity, or the members of the Court of the Bank of England. At this level, the relevant data

---

[123] Pettigrew, A. M. (1979) On studying organizational cultures. *Administrative Science Quarterly*, 24(4), 570–81.

Pettigrew, A. M. (1997) What is processual analysis? *Scandinavian Journal of Management*, 13(4), 337–48.

[124] Langley, A. (1999) Strategies for theorizing from process data. *Academy of Management Review*, 24(4), 691–710.

Langley, A. (2007) Process thinking in strategic organizations. *Strategic Organization*, 5(3), 271–82.

includes the characteristics of each person: their personality, IQ, health, age, gender, race, education, professional qualifications, religion, value system, experience, skills, inter-personal abilities and other attributes of individuals. Psychological, sociological and other behavioural theories might provide insights at this level.

Level 2 contains the governing body itself; for example, the board of a limited liability company, the Council of a University, the committee of a sports club. Relevant theoretical insights come from theories of social networks or class hegemony, longitudinal and other case studies, political economics, or game theory.

The concepts of sociology, political science and company law (stakeholder theory) might also contribute insights at this level.

Level 3 focuses on the governing body of a corporate entity and that entity's members (shareholders, trade union members, members of a co-operative society or members of a professional institution, for example). Relevant theoretical insights come from stewardship theory and the theory of universal ownership, agency theory and related theories of financial economics, including transaction cost economics and resource dependency theory.

Level 4 contains the corporate entity, its independent external auditors and corporate regulators. Relevant theoretical insights come from stewardship theory (company law), trust law or law regulating corporate entities in that sector, such as trade unions, charities, co-operative societies or building societies (savings and loan associations).

Level 5 includes the corporate entity and its contractual stakeholders, including its shareholders, employees, suppliers, distributors, agents and its customers. Relevant theoretical insights come from stakeholder concepts, economics, employment and contract law and the concepts of strategy formulation and marketing.

Level 6 is the level of *all* stakeholders including both the non-contractual stakeholders, such as competitors (local, national and international), communities, government departments, the media, trade unions, quangos and other entities that could affect or be affected by the corporate entity. Theoretical insights might come from stakeholder theory and enlightened shareholder theory, or economics (pricing theory for example), political science and the concepts of strategy formulation.

It might be argued that there is yet a further, higher level, that sees the corporate entity in its societal setting. At this level, issues of relationships between the individual, the corporate entity and the state become apparent. But that seems to be in the field of philosophy, rather than corporate governance.

Recognising that theoretical approaches to corporate governance are looking at the subject from different levels of abstraction provides a useful meta-theory. At each level, academic theoretical perspective offers relevant insights at that level. No single perspective provides a complete picture. Conclusions drawn from research need to be interpreted in the context of the relevant level.

Nevertheless, theory at any level depends on the existence of a corporate entity, which is defined by its own constitution: the memorandum and articles of association for a limited company, the charter of a college or the rule book of a trade union.

9 Rethinking the Joint-Stock Limited Liability Company

I have previously called for the concept of the joint-stock limited liability company to be re-thought:[125]

> Society has lost the control which it originally demanded for the right to incorporate [limited liability] companies. Faced with government support of failing companies, a growing concern for corporate social responsibility and sustainability (and many other contentious issues), the time has come to rethink the rationale, the purpose and the governance of the joint-stock, limited-liability company.

A central thesis of this Element is that nineteenth-century society permitted the creation of the joint limited liability companies only if their purpose was clearly defined and their lifespan finite. But those constraints were soon overcome. Moreover, many in society now question some corporate behaviour. Examples include:

~ calls for controls on allegedly excessive top management remuneration, including golden handshakes, golden parachutes and bonuses that can reward failure not sustained success

~ perceptions of top-management greed reducing shareholder value

~ reported cases of domination by over-powerful directors

~ demands for closer shareholder involvement and closer investor relations

~ growing concerns about over-exposure to corporate strategic risk

~ questioning the role of companies in society, with calls for better corporate social responsibility, sustainability and environmental concern

~ proposals for stakeholder involvement in corporate affairs

~ widespread concerns, expressed throughout the economically advanced world, about companies' effect on the environment, global warming and indeed the survival of mankind

---

[125] Tricker, Bob (2011) Re-inventing the limited liability company. *Corporate Governance – An International Review*, 19(4, July), 384–93.

~ concerns about government support for failing manufacturing and financial institutions. Many people see no reason for taxpayers to be liable for corporate debt, just because these companies are thought to be 'too big to fail'

~ growing interest in business behaviour, ethics and environmental impact.

Some attempts have already been made to rethink the place of the company in society. 'Tomorrow's Company,'[126] a UK not-for-profit think-tank, is trying to encourage a business approach that creates value for staff, shareholders and society through a focus on purpose, values and relationships in the long term. The project's objectives were re-stated in 2016, in the light of twenty years' experience, to develop companies that had:

~ 'a purpose beyond profit and a set of values that are lived through the behaviours of all employees to create a self-reinforcing culture

~ collaborative and reciprocal relationships with key stakeholders – a strong focus on customer satisfaction, employee engagement, and where possible, collaboration with suppliers, alongside working with society

~ a long-term approach that embraces risk

~ investing long term and embracing disruptive innovation.'

A re-engineered company governance model would need to recognise legit-imate interests of all involved parties, including:

~ equity investors with shareholder voting rights

~ other sources of funding

~ the executive management of the enterprise

~ all contractual stakeholders, including employees, suppliers and customers, indeed all those in the up- and down-stream added-value chains

~ other potential stakeholders.

In the nineteenth century, a corporate governance system was created that required companies to meet society's expectations. Today, companies could be held responsible for meeting society's current expectations as the price for limited shareholder liability. In other words, if a company wants limited liability it must meet societies' expectations. Limited liability is a privilege that is granted by society not a right. What society has given it can take away. Power in society should be exercised through its legislators not by companies through their directors. Of course, such a development could only be achieved with

---

[126] www.tomorrowscompany.com
www.tomorrowscompany.com/aboutus.38aspx

society's agreement and subsequent legislation. Recognition of the need to rethink the concept of the limited liability company would be a first step.

The economic, social and political context is certainly vastly different from that of the nineteenth century when the limited company was invented. The number, scale, complexity, diversity and significance of companies are now of a different order.

10 Towards a Philosophy of Corporate Governance

The fourth (2019) edition of my textbook *Corporate Governance – Principles, Policies, and Practices*[127] concludes with the suggestion that it is time that a philosophy of corporate governance was developed. This Element provides an opportunity to pursue that thought. It does not attempt to create such a philosophy, which will require research and thought. Rather, it tries to explain what such a philosophy might include, why it is needed and why it would be useful. Indeed, it would cover all six theoretical levels of abstraction previously mentioned and provide an over-arching perspective for level six.

What is Meant by a 'Philosophy of Corporate Governance'?

Up to now, the dominant contributions to corporate governance thinking, as we have seen, have come from the economic and legal perspectives, what Sir Adrian Cadbury[128] called the 'financial aspects of corporate governance'. He had experience as a director and Chair[129] of the Cadbury's Chocolate Company and appreciated that a fuller understanding would have more dimensions. To date, less emphasis has been placed on the behaviour of individuals and board-level groups; in other words, on the behavioural and political perspectives.

By its nature, corporate governance is territorial, part of the culture, embedded in the belief systems, reflected in the values, politics and laws of each country. A comprehensive and coherent philosophy of corporate governance would have to embrace every form of corporate entity, wherever it was incorporated and operated in the world.

The study of corporate governance to date, as we have seen, has concentrated on the governance of public companies listed on stock exchanges, country by country. A taxonomy of corporate types will be needed. Among limited liability companies, for example, it would need to differentiate public, private, family,

---

[127] Tricker, Bob (2019) *Corporate Governance – Principles, Policies, and Practices, 4th ed.* Oxford University Press, Oxford.

[128] The Report of the Committee on '*The Financial Aspects of Corporate Governance*' (The Cadbury Report). 1 December 1992, Gee & Co., London.

[129] Cadbury, Adrian (2002) *Corporate Governance and Chairmanship – a Personal View.* Oxford University Press, Oxford.

conglomerate, holding, associate, subsidiary, joint venture, non-profit and other types of entity. Ownership structures in complex corporate groups, including those linked in pyramids, chains, nets and other structures, need to be distinguished. The basis of power in academic, arts, cooperative, medical, sports, professional and other institutions and societies would need to be defined.

Similar distinctions would have to be developed for all other types of corporate entity including, to list a few, clubs and societies, charities, professional and scientific institutions, co-operatives, trade unions, education and health authorities, arts, science bodies, social welfare groups, sporting organisations, partnerships of all types and trusts.

A philosophy of corporate governance would outline the fundamental nature of the subject, identifying its underlying ideas and ideology, establishing its body of knowledge and accepted principles, and outline its contributing theories. It would also cover and clarify the various schools of thought currently applied to the subject.

The development of a philosophy of corporate governance could lead to the recognition of corporate governance as an academic discipline, able to stand alongside subjects such as anthropology, economics, history, politics, sociology, theology and the physical sciences.

The Basic Concepts of a Corporate Governance Philosophy

Throughout this Element, 'corporate governance' has been broadly defined as the way power is exercised *over* corporate entities.[130] Under that definition, corporate governance has two principle elements – 'corporate entity' and 'power'. Deeper consideration of those two terms suggests that the concept of 'corporate governance' may cloak some major philosophical issues.

In the fourth century BC, Aristotle laid down rules about how power and authority should be exercised over Greek city-states. *Corporate* governance concerns the way power is exercised over *corporate* entities. Every corporate entity is defined by its constitution or rules and governed by its members, under the law of the relevant jurisdiction.

A '*corporate entity*' is an organisation created under a written constitution or set of rules, which establish its identity, purpose, membership and governance processes. In the case of a limited liability company, the company is incorporated under company law. Its constitution is provided by the company's memorandum and articles of association filed on incorporation. Its members are the shareholders with voting rights, which typically allows them to nominate and elect the board of directors and matters that can be raised at shareholder

---

[130] The exercise of power *within* corporate entities is the subject of management.

meetings. The directors have the power and the duty to govern, in accordance with the company's articles. In a company listed on a stock exchange, the company must also conform to the listing rules of that exchange, and to relevant corporate governance codes. In a private company, the shareholders have the rights and the directors have the powers and duties granted by that company's articles; although, in a closely held family company, some family members may wield more influence than their voting rights suggest because of their position in the family. In a professional body, such as the UK Law Society or the Institute of Chartered Accountants, full members have the rights and the Council has the powers and duties granted by the organisation's charter. In a trade union, fully paid members have the rights and duties contained in the official rule book. In a co-operative, members can exercise the rights given to them by the co-operative's constitution and rules.

'Power' was defined by Mary Parker Follet,[131] many years ago in an all-encompassing phrase, as 'the ability to make things happen'. Various author-ities, clearly, can exercise that authority over corporate entities. Power over corporate entities can be exercised at various levels: by the state in which it is incorporated or operates; by the members of that entity; and by its governing body. The power exercised by and within a governing body may stem from formal *authority*, derived from the legal standing of that body and its members, or from *influence*, derived from respect, privilege or personality.

Corporate governance power can be used to achieve outstanding results: it can also be abused. The politics and ethics of power are intrinsic to corporate governance. However, the evolution of corporate governance owes more to responses to crises, corporate collapses and executive misdemeanours than to research or logical reasoning.

The ability to exercise power over a corporate entity can come from many sources. The shareholders of a limited liability company have the powers granted by the company's articles of association. The members of a club, institution or society have the powers granted by that entity's constitution or rules. The trustees appointed under a trust deed have the power granted by that deed.

The members or shareholders of an organisation delegate much of their potential power to their elected governing body; although some individual members of a governing body may wield disproportionate power through their position or personality.

Independent external auditors, government regulators and other external bodies, such as the stock exchange for listed companies, can wield power

---

[131] Fox E. M. and Urwick, L. (eds.) (1940) *Dynamic Administration: the Collected Papers of Mary Parker Follett*. Pitman Publishing, London.

over entities, as might an administrator or liquidator appointed by the courts. Society at large can also influence the behaviour of a corporate entity, using the law, lobbyists, the media or by exerting other pressures.

The exercise of corporate power in society raises philosophical issues about relationships between individuals, entities and states. None of the theories discussed previously addresses such issues; yet they are fundamental to the acceptable exercise of power. Corporate governance needs a philosophy that is concerned about the corporate entity in society.

This suggests that moral philosophy might have a contribution to make to the development of a philosophy of corporate governance. Such philosophy concerns attitudes, beliefs, convictions, ideology and values. It embraces the ethics of individuals, groups and societies. These considerations would add vital new dimensions to the subject.

People have a great capacity for self-delusion, believing in the superiority of their own system of corporate governance. The United States is committed to legally enforced corporate governance under state and federal rule of law. In Britain and countries in the British Commonwealth, commitment to the reporting of voluntary adherence to a corporate governance code prevails. Germans are committed to their co-determination form of governance with two-tier boards separating management and its supervision representing both labour and capital. While in Japan, there remains a hankering after the traditional practices of corporate governance, despite the recent imposition by government of independent directors on company boards.[132]

The logical reasoning of moral philosophy might produce a rationale for the economic, social and political reality: in other words, provide a logical basis for corporate governance activities, beliefs and values. Such philosophy would need to embrace every corporate entity, whatever its size, purpose or domicile; and differentiate governance from management, reflecting economic, political and cultural realities. Overall a philosophy of corporate governance would explain how power is exercised over corporate entities and suggest how it could be improved.

In medieval times Europe was controlled by monarchs and property-owning aristocrats; self-governing trade guilds supervised crafts; and trading ventures flourished under the patronage of potentates. After 1918, three political ideologies prevailed in Europe: social democracy; communism; and fascism. Despite the prevailing ideology, during the 1930s enterprises were governed in democratic Britain, France and Scandinavia, fascist Germany and communist Russia.

---

[132] Seki, Takaya and Clarke, Thomas (2014) The evolution of corporate governance in Japan: the continuing relevance of Berle and Means. *Seattle University Law Review*, 37(2), 717–47.

Moreover, corporate entities are governed not only in democratic societies. In China, over the past thirty years, enterprises have achieved substantial economic success under a one-party communist state (albeit communism with distinctive Chinese characteristics that involves a surprising degree of regional and enterprise autonomy relative to the rigid centralised Soviet system applied in Russia). Nevertheless, capitalism remains a dominant ideology in the creation of economic wealth in the world.

The Essential Elements of Corporate Governance Power

Three essential elements are needed to exercise corporate governance power successfully: authority; acceptance; and accountability. *Authority* ensures the ability to enforce underlying power, whether that is through the law, the entity's constitution or decisions of the governing body, or authority derived from personal position. *Acceptance* of corporate governance authority involves trust. *Accountability* completes the cycle of exercising corporate governance power by demonstrating that authority has been wielded appropriately.

Trust has always been at the heart of corporate governance. The merchant adventurer trusted the captains of his fleet to follow their instructions. Victorian businessmen sealed their contracts with a handshake. In a partnership, partners trust each other. In a company, shareholders trust their directors. Trust is fundamental to the concept of the limited liability company and company law.

In every corporate entity, the members trust those they have placed in power. They must believe in the ability, the reliability and, above all, the integrity of those given the authority to govern that entity.

In some cases, trust in those given power to govern is reinforced by law (company law, contract law or the law of trusts, for example). But in other cases, those involved with the corporate entity must place their trust in those involved in its governance.[133] But what do we really mean by trust?

> Trust is a central part of all human relationships, including romantic partnerships, family life, business operations, politics, and medicine.[134]

Trust is an abstract attitude that involves believing a person or organisation will act in a certain way. Trust inspires confidence and provides security. Trust is the glue that bonds parties together. Those with power need to be trusted by those affected by their actions. Inevitably, this imposes moral responsibilities, as well

---

[133] Blair, Margaret and Stout, Lynn (2001b) Trust, trustworthiness and the behavioural foundations of corporate law. *University of Pennsylvania Law Review*, 149, 1735–810.
[134] Thagard, Paul (9 October 2018)
        www.psychologytoday.com/gb/experts/paul-thagard-phd

as legal duties, on those with power and authority. The ethical dimension of corporate governance, rooted in basic values such as morality, honesty, integrity, respect, concern for others and, above all, trust, has not been sufficiently recognised in corporate governance studies.

Including an ethical dimension will be a challenge to the development of a corporate governance philosophy. The black box of the board will need to be opened, to focus on directors' behaviour and beliefs, board processes, politics and leadership. The significance of culture, at the national, corporate and board levels, will also have to be recognised.

11 Conclusions

The Evolutionary Process

This Element has adopted an evolutionary approach to reviewing corporate governance, tracing the development of practices, regulation and theories through time. In addition to this longitudinal perspective, studying the development of corporate governance in different countries and cultures has highlighted cultural influences and interactions between countries.

The concept of the limited liability company followed a classical evolutionary trajectory. Once created, the idea was copied and multiplied, in a process that some have called the inheritance of 'memes'; that is the evolution of ideas, mirroring evolution in the biological world through genes. When successful, an idea thrived and multiplied: when an approach failed it died out. Forms that survive and thrive in specific situations are selected in future. As circumstances changed, the concept adapted and split into new forms and different species. The joint-stock limited liability company was originally conceived to attract funds from external investors. When it was realised that limited liability could be gained by family businesses, the private company appeared, no longer needing to raise funds from the public. When it became apparent that companies could own other companies, complex groups appeared, with companies linked in chains, networks and pyramids. Subsequently, limited liability companies adapted to meet the needs of corporate entities with social dimensions, such as charities, academic institutions and hospitals: bodies that did not have a single profit-creating motive. An ongoing strength of the corporate concept lies in the diversity of variety, complexity and structure that is feasible. Of course, as in all species, individual companies differ in their size, complexity and structure.

The joint-stock limited liability company was a creation of the industrial revolution in Victorian England. Today's global instant-information society needs the creation of a governance vision that covers all types of corporate entity. However, the process of evolution can be slow. It took nearly fifty years for the private company to emerge from the original public company model. Subsequent developments have taken less time. Today, new forms of incorporation, structure and function occur frequently.

Moreover, the average lifespan of companies is shortening. In the past, companies tended to last for many years; indeed, their founders often thought they would survive in perpetuity. Now the time between incorporation and liquidation, takeover or merger has shortened. Survival of the fittest obviously applies to corporate species like any other.

A central argument of this Element has been that the original concept of the limited liability company was brilliantly simple and successful, but over time has become complex, confused and sometimes corrupt. Ownership, however, remains the basis of power over companies, whether that ownership is in the hands of individuals, institutions or other corporations. But that source of power base may change in the future:

o as information, stored electronically, replaces money in physical and written form as the vehicle of exchange
o as new sources of funding offer alternatives to stock exchange flotation
o as entrepreneurs and institutions replace individual shareholders
o as access to information and communication becomes instantaneous
o as new sources of power under new elites emerge.

The social historian may show that the nineteenth-century concept of the joint-stock limited liability company ultimately went the way of the dinosaurs.

The limited liability company was a creation of nineteenth-century England; as that country approached the height of empire, was thriving economically and with its citizens self-confident in their democracy, which exercised power over the state and its dominions. The governance companies, based on shareholder democracy, reflected the same confidence.

Today, however, in the United Kingdom, the United States, France and other countries, the superiority of parliamentary democracy is being questioned. Inevitably, democracy produces an elite political class, which can become remote from the people. Similar questions are being raised about the governance of companies. Maybe there is a need to reinvent the corporation, rethink its governance and, indeed, to rethink the governance of all corporate entities in society.

The Relevance of Culture: the Significance of Trust

As we have seen, the dominant contributions to corporate-governance thinking to date have come from the law and economics. Company law has developed, often in response to financial challenges, corporate collapses or prevailing wisdom, supported by corporate regulators, auditors, advisory institutions and, of course, the courts. Insights from the world of economic theory have been supported by developments in financial reporting and the availability of relevant information.

While developments in the law and economics will, undoubtedly, continue, major future contributions to corporate governance are likely to come from the behavioural sciences, political science and ethics. The psychology and belief systems of those involved in governance activities, the attitudes, behaviours and political manoeuvring during and outside meetings, and the ethical implications of corporate decisions are not well understood. The politics of power are central to an understanding of corporate governance.

That corporate governance involves power and is essentially a political process, is not widely recognised. The political dimension of corporate governance processes and the relationship of companies to society offer further fields for development of knowledge. The use and abuse of power in society, inevitably, raises ethical issues, which can also be developed.

In recent years, the relevance of culture to corporate governance has been recognised. However, too often the concept has been used to cloak the lack of precise thinking. Countries have a culture that affects corporate governance in that country; companies develop their own unique culture reflecting their attitude to business and risk; each governing body develops its own culture, usually under the influence of the chair or other dominant personalities. Although these levels of culture interact, they are different, and need to be distinguished.

The pre-eminent concept in all corporate governance cultures is trust. Members of a governing body trust each other, and members of an organisation trust the members of its governing body. The original concept of the joint-stock company was based on trust. The corporate governance codes depend on trust. Trust between the parties involved has been fundamental to subsequent developments in corporate governance structures and processes. Trust is the fundamental dimension for all corporate governance.

Towards a Philosophy of Corporate Governance

The evolution of corporate governance, traced in this Element, has reached a critical frontier in many countries around the world. Company law and voluntary codes now cover corporate governance structures and processes, director responsibilities and corporate accountability for listed companies. The importance of the sound governance of other corporate entities is also widely accepted.

Now deeper philosophical issues are apparent concerning the use of corporate power in society. An all-embracing philosophy of governance for all corporate entities is needed. The Appendix hints at the variety of corporate entities that will need to be covered in that taxonomy of corporate entities. Different sources of power over corporate entities will need to be recognised, showing how they are replacing traditional sources, including shareholder and stock market power. Such developments spotlight the philosophical issues that arise in determining the appropriate balance of interests between individuals, enterprises and states. What is the desirable balance between their respective rights, responsibilities and powers? Opinions vary significantly by country, culture, prevailing political context and the social and legal systems in each country.

Of course, such issues have been occurring and responses evolving throughout history. The governance of societies has always needed systems that established how power was to be exercised and held accountable. But today, the power of corporate entities in society is greater than at any time in history. The future of society depends on corporate power being held responsible for the long-term benefit of society.

Appendix

Towards a Taxonomy of Corporate Entities: a Few Examples of the Vast Array of Corporate Entities

1. Companies incorporated and listed in the United States (e.g. Amazon)
2. Companies incorporated in China and listed in China and the United States (e.g. Alibaba Group
3. Professional associations (e.g. The Institute of Chartered Accountants in England and Wales)
4. French Societé Anonyme
5. Hong Kong Chinese family companies listed in Hong Kong
6. Mainland Chinese companies listed in New York
7. Chinese state-owned enterprises
8. Australian charities
9. Canadian hospitals
10. Architectural and accountancy partnerships.

Bibliography

Accounting Standards Steering Committee (1975) *The Corporate Report*. The Institute of Chartered Accountants in England and Wales, London.

Ansoff, H. Igor (1969) *Business Strategy*. Penguin, London.

Auerbach, Norman E. (1973) Audit committees, a new corporate institution. *Financial Executive*, September, 96–7,102, 104.

Barney, Jay B. and Hesterly,William S. (2008) *Strategic Management and Competitive Advantages*. Pearson, Prentice Hall, Upper Saddle River, NJ.

Baysinger, Barry D. and Butler, Henry N. (1985) Corporate governance and the board of directors: performance effects of changes in board composition. *Journal of Law, Economics, and Organization*, 1(1, Spring), 101–24.

Berle, Adolf A. and Means, Gardiner C. (1932) *The Modern Corporation and Private Property*. Macmillan, rev. by Adolf Berle (1967) Columbia University, Harcourt, Brace and World, New York.

Blair, M. M. and Stout, L. (1999) A team production theory of corporate law. *Virginia Law Review*, 85, 247.

Blair, M. M. and Stout, L. (2001a) Director accountability and the mediating role of the corporate board. *Washington University Law Quarterly*, 79, 403.

Blair, Margaret and Stout, Lynn (2001b) Trust, trustworthiness and the behavioural foundations of corporate law. *University of Pennsylvania Law Review*, 149, 1735–810.

Bullock, Alan (1977) *Report of the Committee of Inquiry on Industrial Democracy*. Her Majesty's Stationery Office, London.

Business Roundtable (2019) Statement on the Purpose of a Corporation. Business Roundtable, Washington, DC. https://opportunity.businessroundtable.org/wp-content/uploads/2019/08/BRT-Statement-on-the-Purpose-of-a-Corporation-with-Signatures.pdf

Cadbury, Sir Adrian (1992) *The Financial Aspects of Corporate Governance: a Report of the Committee on Corporate Governance*. Gee & Co., London.

Carver, John (2010) A case for global governance theory. Practitioners avoid it, academics narrow it, the world needs it. *Corporate Governance – An International Review*, 18(2), 149–57.

Clarke, Thomas (1992) The business descent of Robert Maxwell. *Media Culture and Society*, Sage, London, 14(May), 463–73.

Clarke, Thomas (1993) Case study: Robert Maxwell: Master of corporate malfeasance. *Corporate Governance: an International Review*, 1(3), 141–51.

Clarke, Thomas (2016) The widening scope of director's duties: the increasing impact of corporate social and environmental responsibility. *Seattle University Law Review*, 39, 557–602.

Clarke, Thomas (2017) *International Corporate Governance: a Comparative Approach, 2nd ed.* Routledge, London and New York.

Clarke, Thomas and Monkhouse, Elaine (1994) *Rethinking the Company.* Financial Times-Pitman, London.

Clarke, T., O'Brien, J. and O'Kelley, C. (2019) *The Oxford Handbook of the Corporation.* Oxford University Press, Oxford.

Coase, Ronald H. (1937) *The nature of the firm. Economica*, 4(Nov), 386–405.

Cochran, Philip L. and Wartick, Steven L. (1988) *Corporate Governance: a Review of the Literature.* Financial Executives Research Foundation, Morristown.

Committee of Inquiry on Industrial Democracy (The Bullock Report) (1977) Hansard 23 February, Vol. 380 cc179–355, Hansard, London.

Commonwealth Association for Corporate Governance (November, 1999) *CACG Guidelines: Principles for Corporate Governance in the Commonwealth.* CACG, New Zealand.

Companies Act, VICT. CAP.LXXXIX (7 August 1862) *An Act for the Incorporation, Regulation, and Winding-up of Trading Companies and other Associations*

Confederation of British Industry (1973) *The Responsibilities of the British Public Company: Final Report of the Company Affairs Committee.* CBI, London.

Corporate Governance – An International Review (1993) Volume 1, Number 1, January. Blackwell Publishers, Oxford.

Dawkins, Richard (1998) *The Selfish Gene, 2nd ed.* Oxford University Press, Oxford.

Demb, Ada and Neubauer, Frederich (1992) *The Corporate Board: Confronting the Paradoxes.* Oxford University Press, New York.

Dodd–Frank Wall Street Reform and Consumer Protection Act (2010) PUBLIC LAW 111–203 July 21, www.congress.gov/111/plaws/publ203/PLAW-111publ203.pdf

Drucker, Peter F. (1967) *The Effective Executive.* Harper and Row, New York.

Fama, Eugene and Jensen, Michael (1983) Separation of ownership and control. *Journal of Law and Economics*, 26(June), 301–25.

Filatotchev, Igor and Wright, Mike (eds.) (2005) *The Life Cycle of Corporate Governance.* Edward Elgar, Cheltenham, UK and Northampton, MA.

Fogarty, Michael P. (1975) *Company Responsibility and Participation: a New Agenda.* PEP Broadsheet Number 554, Volume XLI, August, London.

Fox, E. M. and Urwick, L. (eds.) (1940) *Dynamic Administration: the Collected Papers of Mary Parker Follett.* Pitman Publishing, London.

Freedeman, Charles E. (1979) *Joint-Stock Enterprise in France 1807–1867 – From Privileged Company to Modern Corporation.* The University of North Carolina Press, Chapel Hill, NC.

Frentrop, P. (2019) The Dutch East India Company: the First Corporate Governance Debacle, in T. Clarke, J. O'Brien and C. O'Kelley, *The Oxford Handbook of the Corporation.* Oxford University Press, Oxford, 51–74.

Friedman, Lawrence M. (1973) *A History of American Law.* Simon and Schuster, New York.

Friedman, Milton (1970) The social responsibility of business is to increase its profits. *New York Times Magazine*, 13 September.

Grant, Kirkpatrick (2008) *Financial Market Trends (Corporate Governance and the Financial Crisis: Key Findings and Main Messages).* Organisation for Economic Co-operation and Development (OECD), Paris.

Hilmer, Frederick G. (1993) *Strictly Boardroom – Improving Governance to Enhance Business Performance.* Business Library https://librariesaustralia.nla.gov.au

Jensen, Michael A. (2000) *A Theory of the Firm: Governance, Residual Claims and Organizational Forms.* Harvard University Press, Cambridge, MA.

Jensen, Michael C. and Meckling, William H. (1976) Theory of the firm: managerial behavior, agency costs and ownership structure. *Journal of Financial Economics*, 3(4, Oct), 305–60.

Judge, William (2010) Thomas Kuhn and corporate governance research. *Corporate Governance – An International Review*, 18(2), 85–6.

Kelly, G. A. ([1955] 1963) *The Psychology of Personal Constructs (A Theory of Personality).* Norton, New York.

Langley, A. (1999) Strategies for theorizing from process data. *Academy of Management Review*, 24(4), 691–710.

Langley, A. (2007) Process thinking in strategic organizations. *Strategic Organization*, 5(3), 271–82.

Limited Liability Act, 1855 VICT. a. 183, London.

Lorsch, J. W. and McIver, E. (1989) *Pawns or Potentates: the Reality of America's Corporate Boards.* Harvard Business School Press, Boston, MA.

McWilliams, Abagail and Siegal, Donald (2001) Corporate social responsibility: a theory of the firm perspective. *The Academy of Management Review*, 26(1), 117–27.

Mace, Myles L. (1971) *Directors: Myth and Reality.* Division of Research, Graduate School of Business Administration, Harvard University, Boston, MA.

Mautz, R. K. and Neumann, F. L. (1970) The effective corporate audit committee. *Harvard Business Review*, Nov./Dec.

Mautz, R. K. and Neumann, F. L. (1977) *Corporate Audit Committees: Policies and Practices*. Ernst and Ernst, New York.

Means, Gardiner C. (1932) *The Modern Corporation and Private Property*. Macmillan, London, rev. by Adolf Berle (1967) Columbia University, Harcourt, Brace and World, New York.

Mintzberg, Henry (1984) Who should control the corporation?*California Management Review*, October 1, 90–115.

Monks, Robert A. G. (2008) *Corpocracy: How CEOs and the Business Roundtable Hijacked the World's Greatest Wealth Machine*. Wiley, Hoboken, NJ.

Monks, Robert A. G. and Minow, Nell ([1995] 2011) *Corporate Governance*, 4th ed. Wiley, Chichester, UK.

NACD Report of the Blue-Ribbon Commission on Director Professionalism (2002) The National Association of Corporate Directors, Washington, DC.

Nader, Ralph, Green, Mark and Seligman, Joel (1976) *Taming the Giant Corporation*. W.W. Norton Co., Inc., New York.

Organisation for Economic Co-operation and Development (1999) *Principles of Corporate Governance*. OECD, Paris.

Pettigrew, A. M. (1979) On studying organizational cultures. *Administrative Science Quarterly*, 24(4), 570–81.

Pettigrew, Andrew (1992) On studying managerial elites. *Strategic Management Journal*, 13(2), 163–82.

Pettigrew, A. M. (1997) What is processual analysis? *Scandinavian Journal of Management*, 13(4), 337–48.

Pfeffer, Jeffrey (1992) Size and composition of corporate boards of directors: the organization and its environment.*Administrative Science Quarterly*, 17, 218.

Porter, Michael (1980) *Competitive Strategy*. Free Press, New York.

Redding, S. Gordon (1993) *The Spirit of Chinese Capitalism*, Walter de Gruyter Studies in Organisation, Berlin and New York.

Roe, Mark J. (2003) *Political Determinants of Corporate Governance*, Clarendon Lectures in Management Studies Series. Oxford University Press, Oxford.

Schwartz, Robert (1986) *Martin Luther – An Introduction to His Life and Work*. Fortress Press, Minneapolis, MN.

Securities Exchange Act USA (1934) Pub.L.73–291, 48 Stat. 881; also called the Exchange Act '34 or 1934 Act; incorporated into the listing rules of the New York Stock Exchange, and published by them, 1934.

Seki, Takaya and Clarke, Thomas (2014) The evolution of corporate governance in Japan: the continuing relevance of Berle and Means. *Seattle University Law Review*, 37(2), 717–47.

Shleifer, A. and Vishny, R. (1997) A survey of corporate governance. *Journal of Finance*, 52(2, June), 737–83.

Small, Marshall L. (2011) *The 1970s: the committee on corporate laws joins the corporate governance debate*. The Model Business Corporation Act at Sixty Law and Contemporary Problems, 74(Winter), 129–36. Duke University, Durham, North Carolina, USA

Smith, Adam (1776; 1976) *The Wealth of Nations*, rev. edn., George J. Stigler (ed.), University of Chicago Press, Chicago.

Stern, Philip (2019) English East India Company-State and the Modern Corporation: the Google of its Time?, in T. Clarke, J. O'Brien and C. O'Kelley, *The Oxford Handbook of the Corporation*. OUP, 75–92.

Stiles, P. and Taylor, B. (2001) *Boards at Work: How Directors View Their Roles and Responsibilities*. Oxford University Press, Oxford.

Stout, L. (2012) *The Shareholder Value Myth*. Cornell Law Library https://scholarship.law.cornell.edu/cgi/viewcontent.cgi?article=2311&context=facpub

Tricker, R. I. (1978) *The Independent Director: a Study of the Non-executive Director and of the Audit Committee*. Tolley with Deloitte, Haskins & Sells, London.

Tricker, R. I. (1984) *Corporate Governance – Practices, Procedures and Powers in British Companies and Their Boards Of Directors*. Gower, London.

Tricker, Bob (2009, 4th ed. 2019) *Corporate Governance – Principles, Policies, and Practices*. Oxford University Press, Oxford.

Tricker, Bob (2011) Re-inventing the limited liability company. *Corporate Governance – An International Review*, 19(4, July), 384–93.

Tricker, Bob and Gregg, Li (2019) *Understanding Corporate Governance in China*. Hong Kong University Press, Hong Kong.

Tricker, Bob and Tricker, Gretchen (2014) *Business Ethic – A Stakeholder, Risk, and Governance Approach*. Routledge, Abingdon, Oxford.

Turnbull, Shann (1997) Stakeholder governance: a cybernetic and property rights analysis in corporate governance. *Corporate Governance: An International Review*, 5(1, Jan.), 11–23 (also in Tricker, R. I. (ed.) (2000) *Corporate Governance* – The History of Management Thought series, Ashgate Publishing, London.

Williamson, Oliver E. (1975) *Markets and Hierarchy*. Free Press, New York.

Williamson, Oliver E. (1988) The logic of economic organization. *Journal of Law, Economics and Organization*, 4(Spring), 65–93.

Zinkin, John (2019) *Better Governance across the Board – creating value through reputation, people and processes*. The Alexandra Lajoux Corporate Government Series, De Gruyter.

Cambridge Elements ☰

Corporate Governance

Thomas Clarke

UTS Business School, University of Technology Sydney

Thomas Clarke is Professor of Corporate Governance at the UTS Business School of the University of Technology Sydney. His work focuses on the institutional diversity of corporate governance and his most recent book is *International Corporate Governance* (Second Edition 2017). He is interested in questions about the purposes of the corporation, and the convergence of the concerns of corporate governance and corporate sustainability.

About the Series

The series Elements in Corporate Governance focuses on the significant emerging field of corporate governance. Authoritative, lively and compelling analyses include expert surveys of the foundations of the discipline, original insights into controversial debates, frontier developments and masterclasses on key issues. Its areas of interest include empirical studies of corporate governance in practice, regional institutional diversity, emerging fields, key problems and core theoretical perspectives.

Corporate Governance